the DIACONATE in christ

A First Step towards the Restoration and Renewal of the Ministerial Role of Orthodox Deacons in Modern America

REV. DEACON DAVID RENE MASCARENAS

WESTBOW
PRESS®
A DIVISION OF THOMAS NELSON
& ZONDERVAN

WestBow Press books may be ordered through booksellers or by contacting:

WestBow Press
A Division of Thomas Nelson & Zondervan
1663 Liberty Drive
Bloomington, IN 47403
www.westbowpress.com
1 (866) 928-1240

ISBN: 978-1-5127-9036-8 (sc)

Library of Congress Control Number: 2017908920

Print information available on the last page.

WestBow Press rev. date: 06/16/2017

TABLE OF CONTENTS

ACKNOWLEDGEMENT

Special thanks must be given to Marilyn, my wife, who deserves special credit for this work due to her unwavering moral support, her insistence that I not give in to discouragement and her urging me to spend my time writing whenever possible. Without her constant encouragement and her patience and personal sacrifice, this research project and paper could not have been completed.

DEDICATION

To My Family
Especially my Mother of Blessed Memory - Ernestine,
My Father – Ernest,
My Sister of Blessed Memory - Tina,
And My Spiritual Father – Hieromonk Ambrose (Young).

FOREWORD

Our friend and co-worker Fr. Deacon David Mascarenas did not live to see the publication of his edited Doctor of Ministry Thesis. He charged me with the responsibility to bring the project to completion and I honor his memory and his work by joyfully doing so. I regret that pressing circumstances of work in my own life prohibited me from finishing this project until a later date than I had initially intended or hoped for.

Deacon David served as attached deacon with us at St. Anthony of the Desert Orthodox Mission in Las Cruces NM, as he was able, over four plus years before his repose. He served at other parishes in the State of New Mexico as well, most recently also at Prophet Elias Greek Orthodox Church, Santa Fe NM, with Fr. Dimitri Pappas. Deacon David represented in his person the dignity and the sensibilities he sought to restore to the Diaconate in American Orthodoxy. He wanted very much to see the diaconate honored as the full ministry it can be. The text of his dissertation bears out the confusion over the role of deacon that he hoped to overcome in his own ministry and through his work, including this book. The people in parishes he served embraced him with love and respect.

Deacon David's repose in December of 2015 after a brief illness took away a thoughtful and committed voice and presence from the New Mexico Orthodox Churches. David's final two years among us were also marked by a lasting sadness at the loss of his beloved wife, Marilyn.

I edited the work in your hands with a light touch to maintain the intention of Deacon David's writing. To render the thesis as a book, however, required the deletion of a number of passages of purely personal and/or anecdotal nature. Since the thesis was written, there has been almost a complete turnover of Orthodox priests in New Mexico. Only one priest remains who participated in Deacon David's study; namely, Fr John Bethancourt of Holy Trinity, Santa Fe; two deacons, Deacon Stephen Henne and Deacon George Collaros, also remain in their parishes.

Since this D. Min. thesis was written a decade ago, changes in the perception, role, and education of the diaconate that Deacon David hoped for have occurred in various Orthodox jurisdictions, and we tried to reflect those shifts if it was possible to do so in the revision. We hope that these positive changes in the Diaconate, in some way, reflect and honor his work.

V. Rev. Gabriel Rochelle
St. Anthony of the Desert Orthodox Mission
Las Cruces New Mexico
May 2017

INTRODUCTION

I have written this exposition by the grace of God and from the simple fact that I am a student of ministry. My studies have inspired me to become completely dedicated to the restoration of the ancient ministry of the diaconate in the Orthodox Church. In this work, I endeavor to describe the context of my ministry and the research project that naturally ensued from it, and I share the findings of my research derived from this same project. To illuminate and give background to the topic, we will review the scriptures, the teachings of ancient church fathers, the decrees of church councils, the lives of the saints as they pertain to diaconal ministry, and modern works on the holy diaconate.

The diaconate was originally an extension of the leadership role of the Apostles (Acts 6); however, the traditional ministries of the deacon have since been suppressed, distorted or simply permitted to fade away from the life of American Orthodoxy. I can only hope that the entire traditional scope of diaconal ministry will be ultimately restored to the life of the Church. In the meantime, my hope is that liturgical skills can be improved and bridges built to close the gaps in practice among various old world traditions, thus helping to foster administrative unity through common prayer and worship.

May this work be blessed by the Lord for the extension of His Kingdom, for the life of the Church and for the greater glory of God.

Deacon David Mascarenas

CHAPTER 1

CONTEMPORARY SITUATION IN AMERICA AND CONTEXT OF THE PROJECT

Orthodox deacons in America suffer from a lack of understanding about their role and function in the church. This confusion and lack of understanding of the nature and identity of the diaconate is also shared by many among the laity as well as by quite a few among the other clerical ranks of the church hierarchy. There are many reasons for this situation, notably the relatively few deacons that are actually engaged in some form of active ministry in our day. In addition, there is the lack of diaconal experience among bishops and priests, few of whom have served as deacons or have worked closely with deacons as 'brothers and fellow-ministers'. But perhaps the greatest contribution to the problem is the minimalist teaching about the diaconate among modern theologians and the common notion that the diaconate is simply a transitional step toward the priesthood. Unfortunately, church hierarchies perpetuate the status quo – either due to indifference to the departure from ancient tradition or through conscious adoption of the minimalist teaching as a convenient church policy, despite its historical inaccuracy.

All of the above problems contribute to the ultimate problem, which is the dearth of understanding about the diaconate. Here are some examples of this lack of understanding.

Deacons are often looked upon as altar servers and nothing more. In fact, in the Coptic Church (the Oriental Orthodox Church in Egypt) the term 'deacon' a synonym for altar server. I once introduced myself as a deacon to a group of Coptic men and all of them introduced themselves as deacons, too. I was impressed with the advanced appreciation of the diaconate in the Coptic Church until I discovered that they were not ordained deacons but simply tonsured readers who happen to serve at the altar. This, of course, is an extreme example of what can happen to the diaconate if the church fails to exercise this ministry – it atrophies and withers away.

This atrophy is not the case with the Eastern Orthodox Church, particularly in the ancestral homelands of Eastern Orthodoxy. However, there is certainly no guarantee that this will not become the case in American Orthodoxy if this problem is not addressed while the opportunity to do so is at hand.

On one hand, people expect deacons to have advanced liturgical expertise; on the other hand, there has been, until recently, little or no prior instruction. Here is an example of this problem from my own personal experience, one that demonstrates one aspect of this situation. The day after my ordination I was obliged to serve a Hierarchical Divine Liturgy without mentorship from older, more experienced deacons and little prior instruction on how to serve this Liturgy. The result was somewhat traumatic for me and for others watching me make a fool out of myself in the midst of the communal prayer life of the church.

This is not the only example of confusion over the diaconal role and function that I have experienced. Shortly after my ordination I got the impression that certain people in the church did not want a deacon to exercise a viable active ministry to the community beyond a liturgical function - even though seminary training prepared me for pastoral ministry. This impression was made clear by my pastor, my bishop and various members of my parish. For example, I was assigned by my pastor to care for a neighboring mission that had no priest and I was allowed to preach, teach and distribute Holy Communion. This assignment was short-lived and was discontinued when the bishop became concerned that parishioners would become confused over a deacon exercising a pastoral ministry.

Another example of the unwillingness of church officials to allow a deacon to exercise an active ministry is that I was not given a blessing to continue as clergy advisor for a local college ministry program that I founded without any assistance from my parish priest. Similar rationale was given for this decision. According to my bishop's secretary:

> "The parish priest, by definition, would be the leader of any local OCF (Orthodox Christian Fellowship), unless he delegates specific duties to someone else. While an OCF is certainly a campus ministry, the involvement of any member of a local parish, especially a clergyman, in a leadership role makes it a parish ministry as well. As a deacon your primary responsibilities are to your assigned parish. Any other ecclesiastical activity (such as an OCF) requires the approval and guidance of the local priest, and especially the Archbishop. *Vladyka* ("Master" – referring to the Archbishop), therefore, while delighted with your participation in this project, is assigning Fr. George Sondergaard as the spiritual advisor for the OCF at the University of New Mexico".

Unfortunately, the new spiritual advisor did not formally delegate any specific duties to me as required by OCF and University regulations and the college ministry program soon fell into dormancy.

When I studied the scripture and writings of the fathers of the church on the diaconate, I discovered that a restricted liturgical function is certainly not the only way that deacons can serve their local communities. This limited ecclesiological view, coupled with a rigid parochial protocol that renders deacons subservient to presbyters, contributes in a major way to the problem and likely stems from a further confusion between the presbyterate and the episcopacy.

There are other symptoms of the problem. In many cases, Orthodox deacons are themselves the cause of the problem when they think that they were called to serve a priest rather than to help serve the community as fellow minister. Deacons are often taught to act in a manner that demonstrates their subordination to the priest, rather than functioning with a certain amount of independence as trusted and respected co-laborers in the Lord's vineyard.

Contemporary Deacons have forgotten that their office is essentially the same as their predecessors. The deacons of the Great Church of Hagia Sophia in Constantinople, the *staurophoroi* ("cross-bearers"), were often more powerful than higher-ranking clergy. In fact, "a deacon of the Great Church might in fact be promoted in the hope of removing a too forceful personality from the capitol, and should he become metropolitan of a nearby province he would have no excuse for lingering in Constantinople apart from synodal business." Nowadays, generally speaking, Orthodox deacons are not paid and they do not typically serve on parish councils as ex-officio members with voting privileges. Even their wives are often disqualified from eligibility from parish council election, so their influence in local parish business is virtually eliminated.

The same relegation is true on a national and regional level. Regarding national conferences, deacons in the Orthodox Church in America are typically not considered clergy at national church councils. Their parishes do not usually cover their travel expenses unless they attend as laymen. Thus, they are often treated like laymen — even by the laity, who typically call them by their first names rather than using proper clerical terminology such as 'father deacon' or without using clerical prefixes, such as 'Deacon David', etc.

Diocesan Assemblies are somewhat different in that deacons are considered clergy; however, their travel expenses are still not covered in spite of this distinction. The net result is that deacons are often out of touch with what is going on in their parishes, dioceses and national churches unless someone of greater authority informs them. Thus, it is not likely that a contemporary deacon would have the kind of influence in American Orthodoxy as did the likes of St. Athanasios of Alexandria in the First Ecumenical Council or Archdeacon Nicephoros, who was chairman of the Council of Constantinople in 1592.

Since the fall of Constantinople and the later fall of Imperial Russia, the rise of Islam, Communism and the modern age of rapid change, materialism and revolution have all taken their toll on the diaconate. With the decline of *diaconia*, whether through fear of persecution or through indifference, laziness and neglect, the dignity of the diaconate has faded over time. Christendom itself inadvertently contributed to the degradation of the diaconate, as I shall demonstrate. And yet once again, this was partially due to the lack of understanding of the sacerdotal character and dignity of the order on the part of the deacons themselves.

One legendary incident took place in Imperial Russia during the reign of Peter the Great. As the story goes, the Tsar stopped to take the blessing of a clergyman properly dressed in clerical attire – *podrasnik* (cassock) and *riassa* (worn by clergy in major orders and professed monks). The clergyman was a deacon who withheld his blessing due to the fact that he was "only a deacon", which embarrassed the Tsar greatly. To avoid the probability of being embarrassed again, the Tsar subsequently instituted the practice of distinguishing priests and deacons by requiring priests to wear pectoral crosses in the Russian Orthodox Church. Had the Tsar encountered a bold and courageous deacon like the *staurophoroi* of Byzantium, he might well have awarded the pectoral cross to the order of deacons for their legitimate responsiveness to the needs of the faithful.

Now let us briefly examine how this bold assertion can be supported by mainstream sacramental theology.

In the Orthodox Church the bishop is recognized as the ordinary minister of blessings. This is based on Canon 39 of the Holy Apostles, which states: "Let presbyters and deacons do nothing without the consent of the bishop. For he is the one who is entrusted with the Lord's people, and it is from him that an accounting will be demanded with respect to their souls". Nevertheless, Presbyters may bless people, places and things as delegates of the bishop, as is commonly known. However, a case can easily be made that Canon 39 recognizes deacons as his delegates as well. According to regular protocol, a priest can only bless in the absence of the bishop. Thus, deductive logic applied to Canon 39 would indicate that a deacon, theoretically, can bless in the absence of a presbyter if the bishop acknowledges him as his delegate by canonical attachment and if the bishop has enough confidence in his representative to provide consent to his actions. However, the general practice of the church does not always limit the distribution of ecclesiastical blessings to clergy who have been formally delegated by the diocesan bishop. For example, a *Hegumena* or Monastic Superior is commonly recognized as having the privilege of giving an ecclesiastical blessing by virtue of her monastic office. In fact, her authority may or may not have been granted by the episcopate because some monastic institutions are completely exempt from diocesan jurisdiction.

Similarly, we may contend that deacons possess the requisite spiritual gift to bless by virtue of the mystery of ordination, which they have received. The difference is the *manner* in which they bless. For example, a bishop blesses with both hands while a presbyter blesses with his right hand only. Bishops and presbyters both position their fingers to form the Greek letters IC, XC (Jesus Christ), while a deacon would bless as an Orthodox layperson might bless his or her children – with thumb and first two fingers together in honor of the Trinity. Deacons, as we shall see in subsequent chapters, have blessed certain objects, animals and food. This is not done out of disrespect, but is simply due to the fact that each and every member of the church is recognized as a priest by virtue of their baptism and chrismation, or sealing with the gift of the Holy Spirit through anointing with holy chrism. The basis of this understanding is the Catholic Epistle of St. Peter: "But you are a chosen race, a royal priesthood, a holy nation, God's own people, that you may declare the wonderful deeds of Him who called you out of darkness into His marvelous light" (1 Peter 2:9). To the extent that deacons may bless without hesitation, they are conditioned to do so on the basis of these theological and liturgical insights.

Deacons are usually required to be well educated and should intuitively know more than most people about the sanctification of life, time and space as Christ's ambassadors. This is signified when deacons lift the gifts of bread and wine in a priestly offering to God during the Liturgy when the priest says, "Thine own of Thine own we offer unto Thee, on behalf of all and for all". In this case, the creation that is sanctified is also representative of human skill and labor, because it has been worked into bread and wine.

From the very beginning of salvation history, mankind is understood to be the focus of God's creation. "Then God said, 'Let us make man in our image, after our likeness; and let them have dominion over the fish of the sea, and over the birds of the air, and over the cattle, and over all the earth, and over every creeping thing that creeps upon the earth." (Genesis 1:26).

It is not difficult for a deacon to take to heart the moral of the story of the Good Samaritan, which can be found in Luke 10:25-37. The Orthodox deacon knows who his neighbor is without having to ask anyone else. The neighbor is the person he comes into contact with on a day-to-day basis. Moreover, the Orthodox deacon understands the teaching of Christ pertaining to prayer and piety found in the Gospel of Luke: "If a son asks for bread from any father among you, will he give him a stone? Or if he asks for a fish, will he give him a serpent instead of a fish? Or if he asks for an egg, will he offer him a scorpion?" (Luke 11:11-12). Thus, to refer back to the story of the Tsar and the deacon, the moral is not that deacons cannot bless, *per se*. Rather, the moral of the story is that the deacon should have blessed and didn't. By so doing, he missed out on an honor - an honor that went to another class of clergy by default. In other words, he experienced shame and other consequences from failing to act when called upon. Today, in addition to the handicaps here attributed to the incidents of history, the three greatest obstacles the deacon has to overcome in his ministry to respond to the needs of the faithful are ignorance, fear and inertia.

The current state of this problem in Orthodoxy is quite evident in that new deacons are unsure of how to live up to their calling as deacons. On the one hand, they have received the sacrament of Holy Order and are no longer laymen. On the other, they are not presbyters and thus have certain limitations to their ministry as clergymen.

In this paper, I assess the character of the diaconate from scriptural, patristic and canonical perspective, and then outline the proper ministerial role of deacons according to the ancient tradition of the Orthodox Church.

In closing this description of the contemporary situation, I can think of no better summary of the context of my own ministry than the words of His Eminence, Dmitri (of blessed memory), Archbishop of Dallas and the South:

> "The bishop is the preacher of truth, the teacher and defender of the true faith. He is to be the administrator of the mysteries in the church, and the shepherd of the flock of Christ. The priest is delegated in his service by the bishop and is responsible to him in the performance of his duties in the local parish. It is his function to administer the mysteries, preach the word, and to administer the parish. The deacon assists the bishop and the priest in the services and concerns himself with the charitable work of the parish."

We shall now examine the scriptural and patristic record for the means to properly address the problem as it manifests itself in many forms.

CHAPTER 2

THEOLOGICAL DIMENSIONS OF THE MINISTRY OF THE ORTHODOX CHRISTIAN DIACONATE

What is the diaconate? According to professor Fr. Joseph Allen, the diaconate was, and therefore is, "an expansion of the shepherding (i.e., leadership) role of the Apostles", which functioned independently from, albeit harmoniously with, the ministry of the Twelve (see Acts 6).

Let us be clear about the terms. The diaconate is the sacerdotal order of deacon, the priestly nature of which shall be explained as we proceed. The name deacon comes from the Greek word *diakonos*, which literally means "minister" or "servant". This word is used in this sense in the Old Testament: "Then said the king's servants who ministered unto him…" (Esther, 2:2) and "Then said the king's servants who ministered unto him…" (Esther, 6:3). Likewise, we can find an example of this word used in the Gospel: "Even as the Son of Man came not to be served but to serve, and to give His life as a ransom for many" (Matt. 20:28). Also St. Paul's letter to the Ephesians contains another example of the same use of the word 3:7 "Of this Gospel I was made minister according to the gift of God's grace which was given to me by the working of his power".

In apostolic times the word began to acquire a more definite technical meaning. Writing about 63 A.D., St. Paul addresses "all the saints in Christ Jesus who are at Philippi, with the bishops and deacons" (Phil. 1:2). A few years later St. Paul explains to Timothy the qualifications of the diaconate:

> "Deacons likewise must be serious, not double-tongued, not addicted to much wine, not greedy for gain; they must hold to the mystery of faith with a clear conscience. And let them also be tested first; then if they prove themselves blameless let them serve as deacons. The women likewise must be serious, not slanderers, but temperate, faithful in all things. Let deacons be husbands of one wife, and let them manage their children and their households well; for those who serve well as deacons gain a good standing for themselves and also great confidence in the faith which is in Christ Jesus" (1 Tim. 3:8-13).

What was the origin and early history of the diaconate? According to the tradition of the Orthodox Church, the narrative of the Acts of the Apostles (chapter 6) describes the institution of the office of deacon. The first deacons were chosen by the people and ordained by the Apostles, who were to continue to give themselves in prayer and the preaching of the gospel while the deacons took charge of the temporal administration and the assets of the church. In order to respond to the complaints of the Hellenistic Jews whose widows were evidently neglected in the daily "ministrations" (*diakonia*), the deacons were to administer the common goods and see that no widow or child went in need. The first seven were Stephen, Philip, Procorus, Nicanor, Timon, Parmenas and Nicholas.

Besides this material ministry, it was generally understood that there was also a spiritual ministry attached to the diaconal office similar to that of the Levites of the Old Testament (Num. 1:47-54) who administered the ritual of the Temple in a priestly manner. With this in mind, one plausible parallel interpretation of the first half of Acts 6 is that the deacons were to be priestly concelebrants at the Eucharistic table of the Lord and ministers of the word of God. However, in the second half of the sixth chapter of Acts, Stephen (the first of the 7 deacons) is reported to preach and teach with great wisdom and authority. After all, Stephen was certainly well qualified to do so, because according to church tradition the great teacher of the Pharisees, Gamaliel, trained him. Hence, in Acts 7, Stephen delivers an eloquent summary of the economy of salvation starting with the faith of Abraham, the sojourn of the Israelites in Egypt, the account of Moses leading the Hebrew people out of Egypt, the building of the temple in Jerusalem and culminating with a reference to the Righteous One, the Messiah, whom he accused his hearers of rejecting and murdering. Stephen closed his sermon with a direct reference to Jesus as the Son of Man, whom he related as having witnessed, in a vision, standing at the right hand of God, which infuriated his listeners and immediately led to his martyrdom by stoning.

The second deacon to be ordained (Philip) was certainly no less active than the Protomartyr and Archdeacon Stephen. Philip not only served the needy and widows with great diligence, but when the persecution of Christians began in Jerusalem, the Apostle Philip preached the Gospel in Samaria, and there gave witness by many miracles: driving out demons, healing the sick, etc. Such was the dedication of Philip that he was dubbed the "Evangelist," as indicated in Acts 21:8 which says, "On the morrow we departed and came to Caesarea; and we entered the House of Philip the evangelist, who was one of the seven, and stayed with him". In fact, Philip was the Lord's personal choice to enter the area known as Gaza – Acts 8:26. While there, Philip also taught the scripture to a eunuch of Queen Candace of Ethiopia, whom he baptized without hesitation immediately after catechizing him. After that, an angel of God suddenly and invisibly translated him to Azotus, where he taught, preached and converted many to Christ. According to Church tradition, Philip was later appointed bishop of Tralles in Lydia and ultimately reposed peacefully at an old age after a long life of service to the Lord.

In addition to the scriptural record, other authoritative sources from antiquity indicate the actual scope of service for the diaconate in the early history of the Orthodox Church. For example, the Apostolic Constitutions describe an active ministry of deacons as being stewards of church assets (Apost. Const. 2, 27), guardians of church order (Apost. Const., 2, 57), heralds and teachers of the Gospel (Apost. Const., 2, 57), preaching and baptizing with the permission of the bishop (Didache 15.1, 2; Tertullian - On Baptism 17; Didascalia Apostolorum 16), assisting the bishop in celebrating the Divine Liturgy (Apost. Const., 8), and distributing Holy Communion, especially to those who cannot attend the Divine Liturgy (St. Justin Martyr, First Apology, 65).

In addition, deacons traditionally sought out the sick and the poor, reporting directly to the bishop about their needs and following his direction in all things (Apost. Const. 3, 19, 31 and 32). Deacons were to relieve the bishop of his more laborious and less important functions. In this way they came to exercise a certain measure of jurisdiction in the simpler cases which were submitted to the bishop for his decision – especially, but not exclusively, the Archdeacons and Protodeacons exercised this expanded jurisdiction. Similarly, as deputies of the episcopate, deacons sought out and reproved various offenders. This direct access to the bishop and the ability to act directly by authority of the bishop, as distinct from the authority mediated by a priest, stems from the bishops' ordination of deacons: "When the deacon is ordained, this is the reason why the bishop alone shall lay his hands upon him. He is not ordained to the priesthood but to serve the bishop and to carry out the bishop's commands. He does not take part in the council of the presbyters. He is to attend to his own duties and to make known to the bishop such things as are needful" (Apostolic Tradition, 9). In fact, with the permission of the bishop, deacons may impose canonical penances upon minor clergy and laymen for small offenses, but for great transgressions, deacons must bring them to the attention of the bishop (Apost. Const. 2, 44). Likewise, when no priests are available, they are permitted to excommunicate minor clergymen and deaconesses for just cause (Apost. Const. 8, 28, Canon 39 of the Holy Apostles). Indeed, deacons were so closely associated with the episcopacy that they are to be the "eyes, ears, mouth and heart" of the bishop (Apost. Const. 2, 44), or in other words, "his soul and senses" (Apost. Const.3, 19). The Didascalia exhorts as follows: "Let the bishops and the deacons, then, be of one mind; and do you shepherd the people diligently with one accord. For you ought both be one body, father and son; for you are in the likeness of the Lordship" (Chapter 11). Perhaps this is why St. Cyprian recognized the fact that deacons occasionally absolved penitents in cases of extraordinary necessity. Since this is such a radical concept to some, I shall quote St. Cyprian as follows: "...If a presbyter should not be found and death begins to be imminent, before even a deacon, be able to make confession of their sin, that with the imposition of hands upon them for repentance, they should come to the Lord with the peace which the martyrs have desired..." (Epistle 12, 1). According to St. Hippolytus of Rome, the deacon presided at the agape meal if the bishop or presbyter were absent: "And if the faithful shall be present at a supper without the bishop but with a presbyter or deacon present, let them similarly partake in orderly fashion. But let everyone be careful to receive the bread at the hand of a presbyter or deacon" (Apostolic Tradition, 26). This precedent should certainly be sufficient justification for a contemporary deacon to be able to conduct the Office of *Typica* or *Obednitsa* with distribution of Holy Communion from the presanctified or reserved Gifts when appropriate, with the knowledge and approval of the bishop.

Saint Isidore of Seville summed up the various functions discharged by deacons in his 7th century epistle to Leudefredus:

> "To the deacon it belongs to assist the priests and to serve in all that is done in the sacraments of Christ, in Baptism, to wit, in the Holy Chrism, in the paten and chalice, to bring the oblation to the altar and to arrange them, to set the table of the Lord and to drape it, to carry the cross, to proclaim the Gospel and Epistle, for as the charge is given to lectors to declaim the Old Testament, so it is given to deacons to declaim the New. To him also pertains the office of prayers and the recital

of the names. It is he who gives warning to open our ears to the Lord, it is he who exhorts with his cry and it is he who announces peace."

That deacons belonged to the essential makeup of the Church and are therefore of Divine institution is testified by St. Ignatius of Antioch, who placed them in the third rank of ecclesiastical hierarchy: "In like manner let all men respect the deacon as Jesus Christ, even as they should respect the bishop as being a type of the Father and the presbyters as the council of God and as the college of Apostles" (To the Trallians 3:1). This is echoed by the third century document known as the Didascalia Apostolorum, or "Doctrine of the Apostles", which states: "The bishop sits for you in the place of God Almighty. But the deacon stands in the place of Christ; and do you love him. And the presbyters shall be to you in the place of the Apostles" (Didascalia, 9). St. Ignatius also orders the faithful to "give your deacons the same reverence as you would to a command of God" (To the Smyrnaeans, 7) and calls them "ministers of the mysteries of Christ" and "ministers not of meat, but of the Church of God" (To the Trallians, 2:3).

The main point of this examination of the early history of the diaconate is that deacons were fully equipped to exercise their particular forms of apostleship by virtue of their ordination. However, "some have imagined that the institution of the diaconate was at first only intended for the dispensation of temporal goods through social service". Such was the opinion of St. John Chrysostom who apparently thought that the Seven could not be ordained deacons, due to the fact that there were no Bishops at that time (Homily XIV, On the Acts of the Apostles).

Fr. Georges Florovsky based his modern theological treatise entitled "The Problem of the Diaconate in the Orthodox Church" on the view of St. John Chrysostom that the first deacons were not clergy because there were no bishops to ordain them. Fr. Florovsky was of the opinion that deacons are not supposed or permitted to function except as assistants of the officiating priest or bishop, as they are nothing more than liturgical assistants. The brilliance of Fr. Georges Florovsky and the eminent stature of St. John Chrysostom as one of the three holy hierarchs notwithstanding, the views of these great men simply run counter to the general consensus of the fathers and consistent tradition of the Church, as we have already shown. Nevertheless, their views have certainly influenced the Church in terms of the way the traditional role of the deacon has been unofficially suppressed, distorted, or simply permitted to fade from the life of the Church. Evidence of this can be seen in our Orthodox church communities, where the diaconate is still somewhat rare and deacons are typically viewed as specialized altar servers. Likewise, many Orthodox deacons subscribe to the notion that virtually the only ministry that deacons have is serving a priest or bishop during liturgical services. However, this was not so in the earliest years of the Orthodox Christian Church. The Apostles did not ordain the first deacons to serve them, but to help them serve the congregation. Thus, deacons were understood by the first Orthodox Christians to be co-laborers in the same vineyard as the Apostles. If this were true then, it can and should be true now.

Moreover, the first deacons of the Orthodox Church did not hesitate before they exercised their ministry because the Apostles and their successors did not hinder them from doing so. Thus, if the diaconate today is essentially the same office as that held by the Seven, then we should be able to assist our pastors and archpastors to minister to our congregations with the same kind of love and mutual respect that is reflected in our liturgical services. Indeed, if there is a direct correlation between *Orthodoxia* and *Orthopraxis*, then the dialogue that deacons engage in with the other priestly celebrant of the Divine Liturgy, after the great entrance, should apply to all aspects of non-liturgical ministry as well as to liturgical service:

> Priest: "Remember me, brother and concelebrant (sometimes translated as fellow minister)."

> Deacon: "The Lord God remember thy priesthood in His kingdom. Pray for me, holy master."

Priest: "The Holy Spirit shall come upon thee, and the power of the Most High shall overshadow thee."

Deacon: "The same Spirit shall serve with us all the days of our life. Remember me, Holy Master."

Priest: "The Lord God remember thee in His Kingdom, always, now and ever, and unto the ages of ages."

Deacon: "Amen."

In addition to the liturgical and non-liturgical ministry parallel, notice also how the main celebrant humbles himself before the deacon while recognizing an equality and parity due to the Holy Spirit that serves with both clerical ranks together without great distinction between them. This image of synergistic humility is the ideal example of teamwork in ministry involving priest and deacon, both being led to serve others by the Holy Spirit.

There is reason to hope that the traditional role of the diaconate can be fully restored in our day because there are isolated contemporary examples of deacons who function as deacons ought. One of many such examples was described in an article that appeared in the official publication of the Orthodox Church in America's Diocese of the South. In the article we read:

> "The Atlanta area deacons, under the direction of the dean, are serving two of the newest mission stations in Georgia bringing the Holy Gifts and regular services to the fledgling communities and in other ways serving the rapidly expanding mission work of the Southwestern Deanery."

I am particularly proud of the example of the Atlanta area deacons because I served in the Diocese of the South and their example gave me encouragement. It demonstrates the possibilities that exist for deacons within that diocese and, perhaps, throughout the whole of the Orthodox Church in America.

The free and proper exercise of the diaconate can and should bear fruit today as it did in the earliest days of the Orthodox Church, as one of my professors has aptly noted:

> "The diaconal ministry could give new impulse to the community today as it did in the early church, since soon after the ministry of the diaconate was established, 'The word of God increased; and the number of the disciples multiplied greatly in Jerusalem and a great many priests were obedient to the faith' (Acts 6:7)."

To further this end, I refer to two great contemporary teachers who have likewise called for the restoration of the diaconate. Fr. Michael G. Roshak writes:

> "A living and meaningful diaconate is not only welcome but necessary. This diaconate, however, whose liturgical function must be paralleled by community involvement in the parish, must be restored in the light of our 'restored' vision of the Church, and our 'restored' dedication to her life."

Likewise, Fr. Joseph Allen states:

> "What I have been trying to show is that the deacon's ministry can give life to the Church for it brings together the spiritual, social and economic activities of the Church. But this must be founded in love in order to transform it all into something 'offerable' to God. Perhaps it is the lack of such love that has caused the decay of the diaconate. I can offer no solutions to restore the diaconate as it was meant to be, but one thing seems certain, this same lack of love in the Church has caused

the disunity between clergy and laity, the loss of the
social dimension of the Church, and finally, the lack of
a real Liturgical understanding as one of concelebration,
as oneness in mind.

The Church cannot afford to be careless about this, but
when the depth of understanding its own function as the
Body of Christ, 'founded in love and truth' is restored,
perhaps then the diaconate will again be restored."

In closing this summary of the historical resources relating to
diaconal ministry, consider one more biblical passage that underscores
the principal of being a deacon – i.e., *diaconia*. Service is certainly the
underlying principal for any representative of Christ, be they bishops,
priests, deacons or lay men and women. However, *diaconia* is the essence
and basis of what it is to be a deacon. Now I am not referring to anything
less than the Christ's *diaconia*. This is what the church means by the
phrase "the diaconate in Christ" and this is what we participate in if we
are living up to our name and calling as deacons. For this reason, there
is no better scriptural passage to close with than that of Philippians 2:1-
11, the last half of which is an ancient hymn of the Orthodox Church
that ponders the humility and *diaconia* of Christ. Let us then, ponder
the humble model of service of Christ so that we can take counsel from
the holy apostle Paul and be conformed to the pattern of our Lord, God
and Savior, Jesus Christ:

"So if there is any encouragement in Christ, any
incentive of love, any participation in the Spirit, any
affection and sympathy, complete my joy by being of
the same mind, having the same love, being in full
accord and of one mind. Do nothing from selfishness
or conceit, but in humility count others better than
yourselves. Let each of you look not only to his own
interests, but also to the interests of others. Have this in
mind among yourselves, which is yours in Christ Jesus,

who, though he was in the form of God, did not count equality with God a thing to be grasped, but emptied himself, taking the form of a servant, being born in the likeness of men. And being found in human form he humbled himself and became obedient unto death, even death on the cross. Therefore, God has highly exalted him and bestowed on him the name which is above every name, that at the name of Jesus every knee should bow, in heaven and on earth and under the earth, and every tongue confess that Jesus Christ is Lord, to the glory of God the Father."

CHAPTER 3

PROJECT DESCRIPTION AND IMPLEMENTATION

The project implemented toward the degree Doctor of Ministry in 2005 was a two-part educational program designed to address the situation that outlined in the previous chapters by raising consciousness about the traditional full ministerial role of the diaconate, not simply limited to liturgical service. This was accomplished through a straightforward educational process in which I presented the teaching of sacred scripture, the theology of the holy fathers, the example of the saints, and the canonical decrees of the Orthodox Church on the role of the diaconate. Although I had originally proposed a third component, which was to be a diocesan symposium, I did not receive approval for this from my bishop. At that point, I went in search of another venue in the Orthodox Church in America. I met with the chancellor of the OCA, who originally thought the project proposal was worthwhile and the idea excellent in principle. However, the chancellor later told me in a letter dated 07/06/04 that the primate of the OCA thought that the timing of my project conflicted with the All-American Council. "Therefore, His Beatitude is of the opinion that such a program could be offered in 2006. This would allow the Holy Synod and the Department of Pastoral Life ample time to develop and promote the symposium." Since I was already behind schedule due to the Dallas venue cancellation, I met with a regional auxiliary-bishop, who agreed to focus on one important aspect of the project – namely liturgics. Thus, I helped him develop a workshop for deacons and sub-deacons at the Life-Giving Spring Retreat Center in Boulder City, Nevada on February 18-20, 2005. However, I was not allowed to give a presentation nor given time during the conference to gather relevant data for my dissertation.

As a result of this negative experience, it was suggested that I contact the Standing Conference of Canonical Orthodox Bishops in the Americas (SCOBA) for their support of this part of the project. I did so, and am still awaiting their approval and oversight so that the development of such an extensive program can begin.[1] I certainly can see no better way to address the issues identified by my doctoral project than by providing a Pan-Orthodox forum for the free and open exchange of ideas among symposium participants raised by issues that this project brings to bear. Even so, it is essential that my own bishop provide his own oversight and guidance over the ministry of the diaconate in his diocese and over the particular activities of his clergy. As we have already seen, a minor clergyman can do nothing without the knowledge and consent of his bishop (Canon 39 of the Holy Apostles). Therefore, due to circumstances beyond my control, I will not be able to address the problem at hand through evaluation of a diocesan or national symposium in this final project paper until I receive permission to conduct such a symposium. Thus, the deacons and diaconal candidates of the Diocese of the South and the entire Orthodox Church in America must wait to discuss issues pertaining to diaconal ministry in a future educational forum. Perhaps the Diocese of the South will host the proposed symposium for the entire Orthodox Church in America under the auspices of the Standing Conference of Canonical Orthodox Bishops in the Americas as mentioned previously. Then the two objectives can be met at once. Until then, I wait patiently

---

[1] This part of the project never came to pass and Deacon David received the D.Min. degree on the basis of the research that did take place. *Ed.*

because proper protocol requires that my proposal be submitted by my bishop to the primate of the OCA, who in turn submits it to SCOBA for their consideration and implementation. Considering how the wheels of change turn ever so slowly in the Eastern Orthodox Church, we are very likely in for a long wait for a comprehensive continuation of this project. In the meantime, I was able to proceed with this project on a much smaller scale.[2]

The first step toward addressing the problem at hand (i.e., the general lack of understanding of traditional active ministry practiced by Orthodox deacons in America) was through an extensive educational colloquium on the diaconate at the Antiochian House of Studies in Ligonier, Pennsylvania. At this colloquium, I delivered a presentation with the personal blessing of the presiding Hierarch, His Grace, Bishop THOMAS of Oakland, PA. Some brief discussions and an overwhelming response to my initial questionnaires followed this speech. Unfortunately, due to issues relating to confidentiality, I did not have access to the list of conference attendees nor was I able to obtain follow up questionnaires from the senior administrative assistant for the Antiochian House of Studies. This was not for lack of trying, however, as I did ask the assistant to forward the questionnaire to the attendees with a request to return these surveys to me. The assistant agreed to do this for me, but for whatever reason, it was simply not done. Nevertheless, I was able to obtain a significant amount of data from the questionnaires distributed at the colloquium, as we shall see shortly.

This type of collective dialogue would, however, take root and bear fruit in the second step toward addressing the problem – i.e., a locally focused educational *synaxis* on the diaconate. This local focus was completely open to anyone interested in learning about *diaconia* or "ministry" (both clerical and lay) and was to be sponsored by the Orthodox Clergy Association of New Mexico. Due to geographical considerations, this local focus was split into two parts and hosted by my own parish - All Saints of North America Orthodox Church in

---

[2] Since Deacon David eventually came under the omophor of the Ukrainian Bishop, none of this came to pass. I left it in the manuscript for the historical record. *Ed.*

Albuquerque, NM - as well as by Holy Trinity Antiochian Orthodox Church in Santa Fe, New Mexico. The intent was to encourage as much participation as possible among small mission and parish organizations in Central New Mexico.

This two-part project served to educate my fellow deacons and others about how deacons may serve God and His Church (in our own particular ecclesiastical contexts) in a manner befitting to such a high calling. Moreover, this project provided information on the diaconate gleaned through research of the scriptures and tradition of the Church. In this way, it was my hope that we could address the problems of the current situation and move toward a complete restoration of the full diaconal ministry to American Orthodoxy in the foreseeable future.

The objectives of the *synaxis* in my home state was the expansion of the diaconal ministry in my ecclesiastical context as well as the examination of other forms of *diaconia* – including both priestly and lay ministries. The dates, names of the presenters, length and location of each aspect of this project as well as the topics that were presented for discussion are provided in Appendix I. However, some elaboration on the details of the project may still be in order before proceeding to the project evaluation. Therefore, I will base the following description of the local *synaxis* upon diary notes that I gleaned from a video recording of the two events.

On September 10, 2005, my own parish of All Saints of North America Orthodox Church hosted a local conference on *diaconia*. After beginning with Matins, the panelists were introduced. Among these were Archpriest George Sondergaard (pastor of the host parish), Fr. Mario Giannopoulos (pastor of the local Greek Orthodox parish) and myself.[3] Fr. George made the first presentation by welcoming the various visitors and inviting the interchange of ideas as a demonstration of unity in diversity. Although his presentation was supposed to be about priestly diaconia, he proceeded to talk about deacons originally being elected to wait on tables, which by interpretation ultimately referred to the holy

---

[3] Fr. George has since reposed and Fr. Mario no longer serves in New Mexico. He now serves as pastor of Transfiguration Greek Orthodox Church, Ogden, Utah.

table – or altar. He also mentioned the fact that deacons took care of the social work of the church because they kept the purse, so to speak. Likewise, he mentioned that the deaconesses took care of women. The purpose of all of these activities made it possible for the priest to pray. Fr. George went on to point out how he had been quoted in a popular and somewhat authoritative book indicating that deacons are chosen on the basis of having good voices because today deacons do not usually have other activities besides serving at the altar. However, after his recent trip to Russia he noted an exception. He noticed that there were 'full-time' paid deacons that minister as the result of necessity, due to the lack of priests. He then closed by saying that the work of the priest is the fountainhead of the work of the deacon because priestly *diaconia* is the *diaconia* of Christ. That is to say that the priest is to be Christ among us, who makes Christ present through prayer, sacraments and the ministry of the church.

The ensuing discussion showed that contemporary Orthodox views on the sacraments insist that the sacraments belong solely to the presbyterate. Deacons are not permitted to share that function except by pastoral *economia* (dispensation) due to the shortage of presbyters and/or the great number of the faithful over vast areas that need the sacraments. The response from a layperson was simply; "it seems that something is missing". The first round of discussion ended with reflection over the stumbling blocks that lay in the way of the establishment of a permanent diaconate. Among these was the requirement of a seminary education to be considered by the church for ordination to the diaconate which, as Fr. Mario stated, "is an expensive proposition for the privilege of working without pay". Even though there are alternatives, such as the Late Vocations Program in the OCA or the Antiochian House of Studies, the general consensus was that these requirements are more of a stumbling block than a facilitation of vocations to the diaconate considering the type of service that deacons actually provide.

At this point I made my presentation followed by a brief discussion. Among the themes that emerged were (1) the role of a deacon versus the role of a priest in the liturgy, (2) the difference between the diaconate and sub-diaconate and (3) confusion between the episcopacy and the presbyterate. Concerning liturgics, (4) it was noted that the priest does not lead the people in prayer. Rather, he liturgically speaks to God on behalf of the people while the deacon leads the people in prayer, thus making the liturgy a synergistic work of the entire people of God. Thus, traditional Orthodox liturgical understanding has no concept of a private Mass celebrated by a priest out of devotion with little or no response to the needs of a congregation, even though a congregation (or representative thereof) may be present. Each and every role (including that of a fully participatory laity) is equally essential to Orthodox ecclesiology and sacramental praxis. Regarding the sub-diaconate, I pointed out that there is definitely a difference in scope of responsibility between the diaconate and sub-diaconate. After a brief explanation of the sub-diaconate as being a practical combination of clergy and layman, the sub-diaconate was described as typically being a transitional order from Taperbearer (Acolyte) to Reader to Sub-deacon to Deacon.

In the terminology of ordination, two words that mean essentially the same thing were used, but have come to characterize the distinction between minor and major orders. These words are *cheirothesia* and *cheirotonia* in Greek. Both mean "laying on of hands."

Acolytes, Readers and Sub-deacons are minor orders, who receive *cheirothesia* to a non-sacramental clerical office. By contrast, *cheirotonia* is the word used for ordination to a major (sacramental) order – i.e., that of deacon, priest or bishop.

Father George wanted to comment on the part of my presentation that referred to the deacons' direct access to the bishop. He went on to state that, despite the texts I quoted, deacons are not to skip past the priest and deal directly with the bishop, because in the earliest days of the church there was no priesthood – the bishop was the priest. Nowadays the priest is understood to be the bishop in his own parish so the deacon is supposed to go through the priest to the bishop because we have a fully developed hierarchy that must be observed. At this point we turned to the final presentation.

Father Mario Giannopoulos of the local Greek Orthodox Church gave a compelling and engaging presentation on the ministry of the laity. However, he started with a personal example from his experience as an assistant priest. He referred to himself as the worst assistant known to man because he constantly resisted the authority of the *proestamenos* (pastor) in order to assert his own predilections as a priest. Fr. Mario said this because his former pastor finally asked him what he perceived his ministry to be. Fr. Mario responded by stating that we are to be all things to all people. Since Fr. Mario's former pastor thought the role of a priest as more specific, such as spiritual father, or counselor to the parishioners, they had two conflicting approaches to ministry within the same parish. Father Mario pointed out that sometimes we need to be fathers, mothers, friends, babysitters etc. for other people. This is certainly true for priests and it is also true for everyone else not only because we are co-laborers in the vineyard of Christ but also because our ministry takes on various aspects of which we must be cognizant. He referred to the 12th Chapter of St. Paul's first letter to the Corinthians as evidence of this fact and demonstrated that if one's finger hurts, the whole body suffers as a result. He further went on to cite St. Nicodemus of the Holy Mountain who essentially said that we should not look for the reward of men but we should do what is pleasing to God. Thus, if our ministry is pleasing to God, do it – if not, then Fr. Mario suggested that you don't do it. In ministry, there are many possibilities that are open to everyone, so if our ministry is pleasing to God, then we are co-laborers in the vineyard and in time we shall receive our reward, which is our salvation. Fr. Mario encouraged all those present to find their ministries and use them as gifts from God, for "freely you have received, freely give" (Mat. 10:8). In fact, he urged us to go beyond any niche we may find. In other words, we must not limit ourselves to certain functions or ministries that we may find available to laity in the church. We in the ordained ministry cannot do everything by ourselves. We need the ministry of the laity to help us. Then we will become one body and one mind.

The discussion that followed this final presentation varied in theme. The first question had to do with how the scriptural reference (Luke 10:1-11) that was read prior to the final presentation referred to the subject matter of the presentation. The response that I gave was that the scriptural reference was made to the mission of the seventy, who were not clergy at the time they were sent to minister to the people to whom Christ Himself was to go shortly thereafter. Particular attention was directed to the word *axios* (worthy), which is said at the ordination of deacons, priests and bishops in order to demonstrate the correlation of ordained and lay ministries – that is, each person being made worthy by God through the grace of the Holy Spirit. Father Mario, illustrating the great responsibility that is attached to our ministry, remarked how the ordaining bishop tells the newly ordained priest, "receive the Body and Blood of Christ, for which you are entrusted, and for which you must give an account at the Second Coming of Christ". A comment was then made that we get too caught up with what is going on behind the iconostasis but forget about how that relates to what is going on in the lives of the people. The same person went on to point out that the role of the deacon is understood to be a link between the clergy and laity. For example, deacons can say things to the laity that priests find hard to do. The discussion concluded with an observation that some priests see deacons as altar boys and this can lead to resentment and a lack of love between deacons and priests.

On October 15, 2005, this project was repeated in Santa Fe, New Mexico according to the same format as that in my own parish a month before. After Matins, the first presentation was by Fr. John Bethancourt. Fr. John immediately spoke about *diaconia* in the priestly order as he went about discussing Mathew 20:20-28. Cleverly, he mentioned that this pericope gives us 20/20 vision on how to serve in whatever capacity. That is, we must have humility, as this passage shows us that there is no place for egotism in ministry. Christ, who is the model of *kenosis* (self-emptying) invites us to 'humble yourself in the Lord'. He went on to say that there is a right order for ministry. First, we must serve the Lord. If we follow the proper order, we can expect the Lord to bless our food and drink and remove sickness from our midst (Ex. 23:25) and from a place of humility God will lift us up (Jas. 4:10). This accounts for the call of the first deacons, as it is not right to neglect the word of God to serve tables (Acts 6:2). Priests are called to minister unto the Lord through His people (Mat. 25:45). For example, priests minister by washing away the sins of the faithful in baptism and confession, by feeding the faithful the Eucharist, by healing the faithful through the sacrament of unction, and by blessing the faithful.

I started the discussion on priestly *diaconia* by asking the priests to describe a typical day in the life of a priest. According to Fr. John, he only spends an average of about an hour a day on things that only a priest can do. The rest of the time is spent doing busy work like e-mail, etc. He wished that he could say that he was constantly concerned with the one thing needful, but to be honest, the truth is that he has not achieved such an advanced level of spiritual acuity. Fr. Demetrios[4] response to Fr. John was that a priest is a priest 24/7/365, whether he is watching a football game or doing priestly work per se. Thus, if the parish were to pay a priest minimum wage, they could not afford to do so.

I followed this discussion with my presentation, and Deacon Basil Reeves[5] led a lively discussion about the diaconate shortly thereafter. Both Fr. John and Deacon Basil agreed that the full expression of the diaconate was alive and well in their parish, which emerged from the love and *koinonia* between the two of them. Deacon Basil didn't feel called by the Lord. Rather, he felt called by a priest – Fr. John when they were in the Episcopal Church. In those days, he had plenty of experience visiting the sick in hospitals and nursing homes, performing marriages and baptisms. Early on, they mutually agreed that the deacon would do administrative work while the priest does pastoral work. Not much changed after they became Orthodox. Since there is no book in the Orthodox Church that teaches deacons what to do, Deacon Basil simply does everything he can so that Fr. John doesn't have to do it.

Fr. Demetrios responded that there is such a book, but it hasn't been translated. It is called the <u>*Diaconicon*</u>. Fr. Demetrios went on to say that there has been no active suppression of the diaconate and that examples of deacons doing hospital ministry can be found at Holy Cross Greek Orthodox School of Theology in Brookline, Massachusetts. Likewise, deacons in Constantinople can often be seen preaching.

---

[4] Of blessed memory.
[5] Of blessed memory.

The final presentation was given by Fr. Demetrios Demopoulos[6], who began by saying that, the wages that the Lord referred to in Luke 10:1-11 are "whatever we get". He went on to say that the *axios* that is said at an ordination is essential. Thus, the role of the laity in the church is critically important. This is based on the fact that all baptized and chrismated Orthodox Christians are a royal priesthood and are thereby called to minister. Referring to Metropolitan John Zizioulas's book, Being as Communion, Fr. Demetrios pointed out that we are called to offer the gifts that God has given us back to Him. For example, a priest (or deacon) offers bread and wine to God at the great elevation during the liturgy, but it is the work of human hands to make bread and wine out of wheat and grapes. The role of people cannot be underestimated because humans are spiritual and physical beings and their calling in the world is to bring creation into union with God. Therefore, we are ministers to God, to one another and to all of creation. We have our own personal calling within a hierarchical church, but in our baptismal calling, we are all the same and equal.

The discussion that ensued focused on specific roles and functions. For example, people at this gathering seemed interested in such things as the role of music and knowledge of the tones in order to serve as a deacon or reader. Other similar matters of practicality were also mentioned. For example, torchbearers ought to know how to be good altar servers, readers ought to know the services and have good reading skills and good voices so that the message of the word can be effectively announced to the hearer. A discussion about choirs led to the concept of performance, which is generally contrary to the proper understanding of liturgy as being the work of the people – i.e., their worship of God. At this point, the local focus of the project concluded.

Though I was not able to complete the diocesan conference, I still feel that the local *synaxis* on the diaconate made a difference in my local church context – not only for myself, but also for my brother deacons. I will discuss this at length in the next chapter. In the meantime, however, I was generally pleased with the implementation of the project because

---

[6] Of blessed memory.

it finally came to fruition after many different proposals and changes in plans spanning a year and a half. Even when it did become reality, it did not come off without a hitch. Each part had its own unique quirks. As mentioned previously, I was not permitted to contact the participants of the Antiochian House of Studies. Likewise, the gathering in my own parish had twice as many people from outside my parish in attendance as parish members. The visitors were either Eastern Catholics or Non-canonical Orthodox. There were other minor logistical problems that first led me to believe that the project was a 'failure'. In retrospect, however, I have changed my mind about the significance of that event. Finally, the local conference in the neighboring city of Santa Fe was indeed significant, but even there I somehow misplaced the attendance and contact information and began to doubt my ability to conduct follow up surveys. This worry was soon dispelled.

CHAPTER 4

PROJECT EVALUATION AND CONCLUSION

A. Interviews:

I originally hoped to conduct extensive interviews with my bishop (Archbishop Dmitri), the Chancellor of the Orthodox Church in America (Protopresbyter Robert Kondratick), Bishop Benjamin of Berkeley, the Antiochian House of Studies faculty as well as all of the canonical Orthodox parish priests and monastic superiors in New Mexico. This proved to be far too ambitious, so I have gleaned some information about the present state of the diaconate through conversations with the Chancellor of the OCA, Bishop Benjamin, Antiochian House of Studies participants and members of the Orthodox Clergy Association in New Mexico.

In brief, the situation basically stands as I have described it in the first chapter of this dissertation. As one might expect, Eastern Orthodox Christians are primarily concerned with liturgics, as the services are often quite elaborate and sometimes complicated – especially for deacons. This emphasis stems from a patristic dictum, which is an essential component to the Orthodox sacramental worldview – *Lex orandi lex credendi est* (the rule of prayer is the rule of faith). This view is echoed in the teachings of virtually every contemporary Orthodox theologian of distinction. One of the best examples of this is Fr. Alexander Schmemann, who taught unequivocally: "It is my conviction that the Orthodox faith has its most adequate expression in worship and that truly Christian life is the fulfillment of the grace, vision, teaching, inspiration and power that we receive in worship". In the contemporary American ecclesiastical smorgasbord, traditional Orthodox worship with its corresponding traditional theological and anthropological teaching stands in stark contrast to most other contemporary Christian church experiences. The standardization of essential liturgics in the Orthodox Church generally makes it difficult to remain part of the Orthodox communion while engaging in liturgical innovations or heterodox theological speculation. This provides built-in safeguards for faith and worship. But considering our natural preoccupation with liturgical matters, it does make it particularly difficult to focus on anything other than liturgics – even non-liturgical ministry. This is not going to change and that suits me, as I would not sacrifice the safeguards of Orthodoxy for the world. After all, my very salvation and sanctification depend on it. As an elder deacon in my parish rightly pointed out, the Liturgy is an eschatological event. Evidence of this can be seen in the writing of Hierotheos (Vlachos), Metropolitan of Nafpaktos. His Eminence states: "It is noteworthy that in the Divine Liturgy, when we participate worthily and in the whole perspective which this sacrament presupposes, and not magically, we live all the events of the life of Christ and even that of His Second Coming." The only challenge I faced at the onset of the project was to overcome the misconception that the ministry of the diaconate is limited to liturgics.

Another aspect of this situation was revealed by Fr. Kondratick, who pointed out that there are so many variations in diaconal rubrics that virtually every deacon has his own way of serving the liturgy. Thus, there is no standard official way of serving in the Orthodox Church in America. This varies from diocese to diocese and from parish to parish – even though the basics are generally the same. The OCA Chancellor lamented this situation because there should be a certain amount of uniformity in serving so that deacons from all over the country can gather at the All-American Council and serve without confusion.

Bishop Benjamin of Berkeley wholeheartedly agreed with Fr. Kondratick's assessment of the problem. Having spent more than ten years as a deacon, he recalled the fear and anxiety that deacons experienced when faced with the prospect of serving an All-Night-Vigil or a Hierarchical Divine Liturgy. That is why he wanted to help me and agreed to sponsor my project in the OCA Diocese of the West. In fact, he also wanted to facilitate my idea of making an instructional film to address this problem. When I inquired about active ministry for deacons, he referred to the example of Archpriest Matthew Tate in the Diocese of the West, who utilizes deacons to take the Eucharist to the missions in his deanery. At the suggestion of Bishop Benjamin, I invited Fr. Matthew to make a presentation on "an active ministry for Orthodox deacons today and tomorrow" and he graciously agreed to do so. Unfortunately, this part of the program did not materialize, as that would have addressed the very heart of the problem I have identified in this final project paper. Thankfully, however, I found another way to address the issues relating to diaconal ministry, so all was not lost in this aborted venture.

My interviews later continued with the faculty of the Antiochian House of Studies. I discovered a big difference in the extent of diaconal ministry in the Antiochian Archdiocese versus the OCA. One faculty member, for example – Fr. Michael Najim – encourages his deacons to preach regularly, to teach religious education courses, to take the Holy Gifts (Communion) to the hospitals and shut-ins, to conduct parish business and to give counsel to catechumens and parishioners as leaders in the community. I also discovered from other House of Studies participants that this is not uncommon in various regional dioceses of the Antiochian Archdiocese.

I concluded my interviews with the members of the New Mexico Clergy Association. Generally speaking, they all had trouble recognizing the problem for one reason or another. For example, my pastor felt that the deacons' ministry is to serve the liturgy or to do whatever the priest instructs him to do. Fr. John Bethancourt didn't recognize the problem because his deacon and parishioners do not hesitate to provide active service to others. Fr. Mario Giannopoulos also did not recognize the problem for similar reasons, as his deacon had served with distinction for some 20 years. More importantly, he thought that there is nothing barring us to do whatever needs to be done. His fearlessness and determination in the face of adversity has always been an inspiration to me. Deacon Stephen Henne agreed wholeheartedly with Fr. Mario on this point as he felt that any Orthodox Christian can do virtually anything that needs doing, but that deacons can and should do much more than laymen – both liturgically and otherwise. Fr. Demetrios also tended to follow this line of thought as his experience at Holy Cross Greek Orthodox School of Theology was such that deacons were called upon to take care of the faithful, even more so than priests, especially through hospital visitations. He insisted that since the diaconate has not been suppressed, it doesn't need restoring and deacons are free to do whatever the parish priests permit them to do. Since this was an interview rather than a debate, I accepted their views at face value and left the discussion of these views for the appropriate time – after the presentations. This allowed me to compare the survey responses with the interview information in order to discern any significant developments in thought as evidence that my project raised the consciousness with regard to diaconal ministry among those who participated in the event.

B. Surveys:

I utilized surveys to take into account the situation as it existed at the time of the project. These were developed for three categories of participants and were distributed to the following people at the project:

1. Bishops, Priests and Monastics
2. Deacons and Diaconal Candidates
3. Laymen and Women

The surveys were intended to evaluate the entire content of the presentations and the discussions they spawned. Thus, the surveys were given out during the project (in Albuquerque they were distributed at the beginning, while in Santa Fe they were distributed near the end) and were collected before the participants broke for lunch. In addition, the participants were challenged to learn something new about *diaconia* in general, and the diaconate in particular as well as to put this information to good use in their own ecclesiastical contexts. Hence, follow-up questionnaires were also utilized to evaluate whether or not the presentations made a lasting impression upon the people who attended and whether any of the project objectives were achieved.

The three categories of participants, coupled with the three different events that were held, allowed me to triangulate the results of the project twice over. For example, in each venue my questionnaires enabled Bishops, Priests and Monastics to express their views and policies on diaconal ministry as well as lay-ministries. Deacons were able to record their views and experiences while Diaconal Candidates were able to articulate their understanding of the diaconate in the surveys. Finally, laymen and women were equally given an opportunity to evaluate the need for additional ministry in their churches, whether from clergy or from the laity and even challenge themselves to get involved by volunteering their services to the parish community. I will now report and evaluate the results of each of the three components of this project.

C. Results of the Antiochian House of Studies Colloquium:

Out of eighty-three registered House of Studies students, including twenty-five seminarians, there were sixty-six who responded to my initial survey. Among these were one bishop, nine priests, eleven deacons, twenty-three diaconal candidates, nineteen laymen and three women. The Antiochian House of Studies survey respondents represent the following jurisdictions: Antiochian Orthodox Christian Archdiocese of North America, American Carpatho-Russian Orthodox Diocese of the USA, Bulgarian Orthodox Church, Greek Orthodox Archdiocese of America, Greek Orthodox Patriarchate of Alexandria, Ukrainian Orthodox Church of the USA, Russian Orthodox Church

Abroad, Serbian Orthodox Church in the USA, Romanian Orthodox Archdiocese in America and Canada, and the Orthodox Church in America. The variety of this survey represents an excellent cross-section of American Orthodoxy.

Among the first category, the presiding bishop's answers deserve special attention because he was the only bishop present and they may reflect a certain standard in the Diocese of Oakland and the Eastern Region of the Antiochian Archdiocese. Firstly, His Grace considers the diaconate to be a permanent order because, as he states, "we need deacons to serve." He also has allowed a deacon to serve Typika for his community on many occasions when no priest is available. When this occurs, the deacon vests but does not cense; however, he is permitted to distribute Holy Communion. Likewise, the deacon is permitted to take the Eucharist to hospitals and shut-ins. The deacon is also permitted to preach using his own sermon compositions whenever possible. According to His Grace, the deacon has a spiritual father other than his pastor, and he, in turn, is permitted to provide regular spiritual direction to anyone. The deacon does serve as an ex-officio member of the parish council. Moreover, some of the deacons receive various amounts of compensation for their service. His Grace went on to say that parish deacons have not attended national church conferences as delegates but have sometimes attended diocesan assemblies as clerical delegates. Deacons are expected to serve as many services as possible, although it should be noted that weekday services do not prescribe the service of a deacon. Finally, the bishop of Oakland mentioned that his deacon visits the sick and feeds the poor and His Grace emphatically rejects the idea that there are aspects of the ancient role of the diaconate that are no longer appropriate.

Nine priests rounded out the first category of participants. The jurisdictional makeup of these is as follows: four Antiochian, one Russian Church Abroad, one OCA, two Serbian and one Ukrainian. Of these, three did not respond in depth noting that they did not have a deacon in the parish. Seven answered the open question regarding the diaconate as being either transitional or permanent, depending on the calling. Two did not respond to this question. Regarding Typika, all six priests who have deacons in their parishes indicated that they allow deacons to serve Typika during their absence. Most of these deacons have been doing so on several occasions. But in one case, this happens every Sunday due to a special Hispanic missionary outreach program conducted in that parish. Without exception, these priests allow the deacons to vest, cense, preach their own sermons and all except one allow them to distribute Holy Communion. All of the priests indicated that their deacons are allowed to teach the faith to others formally at bible studies, adult education classes and college campus speeches or retreats. All of the priests allow their deacons to take the Holy Gifts to hospitals or shut-ins. Four out of six of the priests indicated that their deacons have spiritual directors other than themselves. Likewise, five out of six deacons' wives had spiritual directors other than their parish priest. Interestingly, only two indicated that they allow their deacons to provide spiritual direction to anyone on a regular basis. Regarding the question about ex-officio status on parish council, four priests said 'no' and two said 'yes', although one of the priests without a deacon said that the deacon would be if he had one in his parish. Regarding compensation for the deacons in these six parishes, half of those deacons receive some form of monetary compensation and the other half are not compensated. Five of the six priests indicated that their deacons have attended national church conferences and two of these (Serbian and Ukrainian) specifically stated that the deacon is considered as a clergy delegate in those circumstances. Similarly, five out of six priests indicate that their deacons attend diocesan assemblies and the same five out of six considered the deacons clergy delegates under those circumstances. All six priests expect their deacons to serve an average of two services a week. For the most part, the data received from these nine priests ceased at this point, with a few noteworthy exceptions. One priest indicated that his deacon is involved with missionary work. Although most stated that they didn't feel that there are any aspects of the ancient role of the diaconate that are no longer appropriate, one priest stated his ambivalence. He said, "Hard to say. Though I believe deacons should have a broader ministry than currently, I'm not convinced they should appropriate all the responsibilities they once had. The church is not static. Bishops were once married, for example, and the church had no deacons at first. So if we argue that we should 'go back', the question is, 'how far back'." Another priest (Antiochian) indicated that, "every church must have no less than two deacons". And finally, one priest admitted that there is a need for additional ministry in his ecclesiastical context. He explained that there is a need (for deacons) "to assist the priest ministerial (i.e., liturgical, pastoral) outreach."

The second category of participants consists of deacons and diaconal candidates. Of the thirty-four total participants, eleven were deacons. The jurisdictional makeup of these is as follows: eight Antiochian, one OCA, one Albanian OCA, and one Ukrainian. Of these eleven, only four are 'cradle-Orthodox'. Curiously, one Antiochian deacon had previously served in the OCA and an OCA deacon had previously served in the Antiochian Archdiocese. Equally curious is the fact that six serve in missions whereas five serve in parishes. Generally speaking, parishes have larger congregations, own property and have been self-sustaining for a longer period of time. All but three deacons had been ordained in 2005 and all had been deacons for less than five years. The average age of these eleven deacons was 46 with the youngest age being thirty-five and the eldest being sixty-one. All eleven deacons are married and all eleven have children – an average of two per household. The deacons who participated tended to be well educated, with three having undergraduate degrees and eight with graduate level degrees. Only two had graduated from accredited seminaries, however. Most support their families as professionals of various types, professor, musician, project manager, attorney, civil engineer, programmer, chemist, and government analyst. However, one person is retired, another is a parish administrator and only one is a seminarian. This background information should help to put the following responses into perspective.

The first question concerned the diaconate being permanent or transitional. Interestingly, three considered it transitional; three considered it permanent and five thought it is neither. Everyone's response seemed personal. For example, those that considered the diaconate to be transitional have a sense that they will be ordained to the priesthood someday. Those who considered it to be permanent have either no desire or no plan to become a priest. Those that rejected both extremes seemed to be uncertain about what the future holds for them; one deacon has yet to discern the will of God for him, another hasn't decided what he desires to do going forward, and two others have left this in the hands of their bishops. Only one specifically stated that he loves being a deacon and considers it part of his identity. For this person, the question is not about the future. Rather, he seems to be concerned about a deeper ontological issue. That is, he concerns himself with the here and now: "I am now a deacon. It takes all of my attention. I think my bishop plans to ordain me within a year or two, but that is his will. I am too busy to concern myself with that. I love being a deacon. It is who I am."

With regard to the question about Typika, ten deacons have served various times. Ironically, only the seminarian deacon had no prior experience presiding over a service in a leadership role. By the same token, the sole seminarian had never preached a sermon, taken the Holy Gifts to the hospitals or shut-ins, or offered spiritual counsel to anyone. Hopefully, he will get this training and experience in his final two years of seminary because the needs of the community can be quite challenging and may prove to be too much to bear for the unprepared. By contrast, the other ten deacons who serve Typika do so vested and eight of them cense and preach their own sermons. Seven of them distribute Holy Communion and have occasion to teach the faith to others. Four of these ten deacons have taken the Holy Gifts to hospitals or shut-ins and one has previous experience baptizing.

Spiritual direction may indicate a certain measure of trust that exists between a pastor and his deacon as well as a sign of respect given to a deacon as a co-laborer. It also indicates a certain level of maturity (or spiritual eldership) on the part of the deacon as it is presumed that one cannot give what one has not received. Moreover, having confessors other than one's pastor can be critically important for deacons and their family members in order to avoid the potential for conflict of interest and the forfeiture of objectivity regarding matters directly relating to the relationship between a priest and a deacon attached to his parish. Thus, it is interesting to note that five of the eleven deacons have a spiritual father other than their parish priest. However, only three of the deacons' wives and only one of their children have their own spiritual directors. Five deacons also provide spiritual direction to others – though, it is not the same five deacons who have their own spiritual fathers.

Regarding involvement in parish business, it is interesting that seven of the eleven deacons polled serve on their parish councils as ex-officio members. Of these, only four have a vote and one in particular is the parish treasurer by constitution, while the other three ex-officio positions seem to be honorary or advisory in nature. Likewise, only one deacon has attended a national church conference, but he was not a clergy representative at that gathering. Four of these deacons have attended diocesan assemblies and three of these are afforded clergy status at these meetings. This is significant because clergy status allows his travel expenses to be covered by the parish. Speaking of finances, only four of the eleven deacons are compensated for the services they provide to their communities. Considering how much service has already been identified, it is good that this survey is anonymous. Otherwise, if specifics were to be become public, certain church institutions might be accused by the civil authorities for defrauding laborers of their rightful wages in much the same way that secular business organizations would be cited for cited for doing so. Never-mind the temporal authorities, defrauding laborers of their wages is considered to be a sin that cries to Heaven for vengeance – see James 5:4. Having stated this important point in a hyperbolic manner, I would further comment by emphasizing the fact that the diaconate should not be a source of free labor, nor should church officials abuse the volunteerism that is offered by its members out of love and dedication. With all due respect, I firmly believe that every deacon should be paid something as an incentive to do as much as possible for the church, and as a concrete means of affirming the deacon's ministry. A little bit can go a long way because deacons, more often than not, have other perfectly legitimate means at their disposal to earn a living. But no honorarium or stipend whatsoever is contrary to our Lord's assertion that "the laborer is worthy of his wages" (Luke 10:7). Hopefully church officials will ultimately recognize this part of the problem and establish a fair and reasonable compensation scale for all deacons based upon education, experience, honors, vocational skills and scope of ministry.

I will now close the review of the deacons' responses with their own commentary. One deacon lamented that "the role of a deacon varies so much between priest to priest and jurisdiction to jurisdiction that some consistency would be nice". Another deacon who preaches, teaches, serves three services a week, communes the sick and provides spiritual direction under the guidance of the priest, said that the thesis of this project "wouldn't change the way in which he serves at all because he is already doing most of these things". Finally, one deacon suggested that, "There is nothing to keep a deacon from fulfilling his call completely. Who stops us from spreading the word, doing charity and serving the poor? Only ourselves. There is too much to be done."

The evaluation of the second category of participants continues with diaconal candidates. Since there were twenty-three who responded, I will condense their responses to highlight the most significant findings for the sake of brevity. Considering that many of the issues directly related to the diaconate were not answered, it shouldn't be too difficult to summarize. The jurisdictional representation of these diaconal candidates is as follows: fourteen Antiochian, three Greek, two Ukrainian, one Bulgarian, one Carpatho-Russian, one Romanian, and one OCA. Of these, seven thought that the diaconate is permanent, four thought it to be transitional and four thought it is neither. The rationales for their responses were based on whether they felt a calling to become a deacon or a priest. Those that felt that the diaconate is neither one nor other extreme typically didn't explain their responses except for one who stated, "I am a beginner". I interpret this to mean that he will discern this matter as he grows in Christ but neither polar extreme is currently relevant to him. Moving on to the life of the church, I found it quite interesting that seven Subdeacons and Readers have permission to conduct Typika for their communities on occasion. Of these, five of them are permitted to preach their own sermons. Most of the diaconal candidates (13 out of 23) are religious educators of one sort or another. In closing this summary, I will relay a few comments made by the diaconal candidates. Two candidates flatly rejected the idea that certain aspects of the ancient role of the diaconate are no longer appropriate. One of them insisted just the opposite by stating; "All of them are appropriate – we need them". With respect to the need for additional ministry in their respective church contexts, one person noted the need for a Spanish-speaking clergyman for a Hispanic mission. Another person noted the need for Orthodox Christian Fellowship outreach at colleges and universities with no parishes. Finally, one person from Africa noted that "there is only one Orthodox priest in the whole province, so the deacon is needed in the church to fulfill a far greater role than just a server".

The final category of participants from the Antiochian House of Studies is that of laymen and women. There were nineteen laymen and three women responding to the project survey. Unfortunately, the survey at the time of the Antiochian House of Studies wasn't fully developed enough to identify the jurisdictional background of the laity. In any case, it is significant to note that among the laymen, twelve already knew that laymen and women are permitted to minister in various official capacities in the Orthodox Church prior to attending the conference, however; seven were not aware of that fact. Most of the laity have occasion to formally teach the faith to others. In fact, fifteen of the nineteen men teach and all three of the women teach. Fourteen men and one woman think deacons should be ex-officio members of the parish council by virtue of their position as deacon. Two out of three women thought that deacons should be paid but only six out of nineteen men thought so. Fifteen men and three women felt that parishes should cover travel expenses of deacons who travel to national conferences. Very few laymen (four) and only one woman have attended a national conference as a delegate of their parish. In some cases, the parishes they represented did not cover their travel expenses. This was the case for two of the four men who had attended conferences as delegates. Most of the men polled (fifteen) and all three women felt called by God to serve the church as lay people. Eleven of the fifteen men felt supported in exploring their ministry and two of the three women felt supported in the same manner. No one expressed a feeling of being exploited or pressured by church officials to serve against their will. In fact, fifteen of the nineteen men felt that their lay-ministries were affirmed, as did all three women polled. Likewise, all three women felt that their opinions are valued and supported, while only thirteen of the nineteen men felt that way. No one expressed any objections to the ancient role of the deacon as it was presented to them. Two out of three women polled thought that the office of deaconess should be restored, while a similar ratio of fourteen out of nineteen men thought the female diaconate should be restored. Curiously, only one woman felt the need for additional ministry in their communities, while seven of the men perceived such a need.

Before moving on to the results of the local focus of the project, I would like to quote a few comments that were offered by some of the laity. Unfortunately, only one woman offered her commentary, but it was responsive and to the point. In response to the question of whether the order of deaconess should be restored, one woman simply said; "Absolutely. The priest is spread too thin trying to serve a large parish". Thus, she naturally felt that there is a need for additional ministry in her ecclesiastical context – "more religious education", in particular. One man responded to this question in a similar manner. He said, "The biggest issue is that the priests, for various reasons, want to do everything themselves – claiming no help, but when offered, we are told not to do anything." Likewise, another man said, "I feel that church-educated lay-people can serve the church as teachers and, with special training, serve many social and educational needs of the church". Interestingly, quite a few men had very positive things to say about the restoration of the order of deaconess. For example, one man said; "Yes, it would be of great value for women to have an official role. The women saved the church in Russia. There is a resource that the church cannot afford to ignore". Yet another said: "Yes, it brings in more workers into the vineyard of the Lord and also may answer the many questions women have about their role in the church". Finally, along the same lines, one man said: "Yes, it is mentioned in scripture and in the Great Church. It is part of the deposit that we have received and it is also a guard against misconceptions".

By way of analysis, I think we can conclude from reviewing

the results of the Antiochian House of Studies colloquium that the participants overwhelmingly agree that *diaconia* is not only important, but that it is particularly important that deacons be allowed to be deacons. Again, it is unfortunate that I was not able to get follow up data to analyze. However, the significance of this part of the project allowed for a broadened perspective on the diaconate that is national and even international in scope. Moreover, the sheer volume of data collected at the colloquium, which already recognizes diaconal ministry for what it really is, is significant even without the added benefit of follow up data analysis. Now let us see how this data compares with the local focus of the project.

D. Results of the Synaxis in Albuquerque:

As with the colloquium at the Antiochian House of Studies, the first category to observe is that of bishops, presbyters and monastics. In Albuquerque there were no bishops present and the monastics that were present either responded as deacons or as laymen and women. Therefore, I shall report the results of the three presbyters who were present – two of whom were Orthodox and one who was Byzantine Catholic. Due to the direct bearing on the situation I related in the first chapter, special attention will be given to the responses of my pastor. Like me, my pastor is a convert from Roman Catholicism.[7] He served as a deacon for one day before he was ordained to the presbyterate in 1977. He is married and has many children and grandchildren. According to his survey response, my pastor did not graduate from a seminary but completed a program comparable to the Antiochian House of Studies in 1960. My pastor considers the diaconate to be both permanent and transitional, citing that "some go through the order and some stay". He has allowed deacons to serve Typika for his community on ten previous occasions. In the absence of the priest he allows the deacon to vest, cense and preach, "if blessed to do so". According to my parish priest, this deacon composes his own sermons "sometimes" but does not distribute Holy Communion. He goes on to say that his deacon has the occasion

---

[7] This was Fr. George Sondergaard (of blessed memory).

to teach the faith to others "if accepting the responsibility to teach under pastoral guidance". He does not seem to know whether or not this deacon has ever taken the Holy Gifts to hospitals or shut-ins. He is aware that his deacon and his deacon's wife have spiritual directors other than their pastor. According to my parish priest, this deacon is permitted to provide spiritual direction to anyone on a regular basis "if blessed". To his knowledge, his deacon has not blessed anything and he is not an ex-officio member of his parish nor does he receive any clergy compensation. Although Subdeacons, Readers and their family members were not eligible in previous years to be elected and serve on the parish council, my parish priest indicated that they are now eligible and may now serve in this capacity. Meanwhile, however, deacons' wives are still deemed to be ineligible to be elected to the parish council as of the writing of this discourse even though the deacons do not serve as ex-officio parish councilors. According to my parish priest, deacons are "not allowed" to attend national church conferences as a clergy delegate. Likewise, my pastor related that his deacon has attended diocesan assemblies as a deacon although he was not considered a clergy delegate at such events. My parish priest expects his deacon to serve "all" of the services on a weekly basis. My pastor feels that "waiting on tables" is one aspect of the ancient role of the diaconate that is no longer appropriate. Finally, my parish priest admits that there is need for additional ministry in his parish – namely, "the need for more outreach to those outside the parish and those within".

The next set of responses come from a Byzantine Catholic priest. This priest considers the diaconate to be either a transitional or permanent order because in Catholic Churches both options exist. This priest has allowed his deacon to serve Typika for his community many times. When this occurs, the deacon vests, censes and distributes Holy Communion – although he does not preach. However, the deacon has preached on other occasions, which were not identified in the survey. According to this priest, the Byzantine Catholic deacon has the responsibility of formally teaching the faith to others during a weekly bible study. His deacon has not baptized anyone personally, to his knowledge. However, two other deacons did baptize in his presence for family members. The Byzantine Catholic deacon is allowed to take the Holy Gifts to hospitals and shut-ins. This deacon has a spiritual director other than his pastor and he is allowed to provide spiritual direction to others on a regular basis without restriction. The deacon is an ex-officio member of the parish council but does not receive compensation for being a clergyman. The Byzantine Catholic priest also expects his deacon to serve at all liturgical functions each week. Finally, the deacon has attended national and diocesan conferences as a clergyman. The Catholic priest closed by stating that the way in which his deacon serves his community is always evolving, so the possibility for change as a result of this gathering is possible.

The third priest thought that the diaconate is both transitional and permanent, depending on the specific needs of the church. This priest has allowed his deacon to serve Typika for his community for over ten years. When doing so, the deacon vests and censes but does not preach or distribute Holy Communion. The Greek Orthodox deacon is able to formally teach the faith through various parish programs. He has also taken the Holy Gifts to hospitals and shut-ins and is allowed to provide spiritual direction to others without restriction. The Greek deacon is not an ex-officio member of the parish council and he does not receive clergy compensation. However, the deacon has attended national and diocesan conferences as a clergyman. The Greek priest didn't have any comments, other than to point out that he does not think that there are any aspects of the ancient role of the diaconate that he feels are no longer appropriate.

The next category of participants in this *Synaxis* is that of deacons and diaconal candidates. However, there being no diaconal candidates present, I will now follow with the responses of Deacon George Collaros. Deacon George was not able to attend the gathering; however, I met with him personally to discuss the content of my presentation and to interview him about his 20+ years' experience as a deacon. By way of a brief introduction, Deacon George was ordained in 1983, is widowed and the father of three and grandfather of two. He has an MBA from Harvard but did not attend seminary – although he wanted to at one point. Besides serving as a deacon in the local Greek Orthodox parish, he is the Chief Operating Officer for a small consulting company. Deacon George responded to the question concerning the diaconate being transitional or permanent stating that it is "neither because transitional or permanent are not canonical options". However, during my interview with him he agreed that some deacons go on to become priests and others do not, but said that, in cases like his own, neither term applies. Deacon George went on to point out that he typically serves Typika three to four times a year. When he does, he vests in Rasson and Orarion, he censes and he preaches his own sermons. He also distributes Holy Communion, but only with the permission of the bishop. Deacon George has formally taught the faith to others at Sunday school, parish council, youth groups and upon invitation to present the Orthodox faith to other denominations. Deacon George has taken the Holy Gifts to hospitals and shut-ins. Deacon George has blessed icons, crosses, houses and means of travel with permission. Deacon George states that he is an ex-officio member of the parish council but that the Greek Orthodox Archdiocese does not permit him to cast a vote. Deacon George has attended regional diocesan conferences as a deacon and is recognized as a clergyman at such events. Deacon George relates that he attends as many services as his schedule permits and he believes he has been fulfilling the traditional role of a deacon. He does not feel that there are any aspects of the traditional role that are no longer appropriate. In fact, he states that "we are more needed than ever to provide balance in the worship services and in the life of the parish, and to support our brothers and co-celebrants, the priests and bishops". Deacon George says that the content of this project deepens his appreciation of *diaconia*. Finally, Deacon George explains that there is a need for additional ministry in his own church context because he has not been able to devote the time he has in the past to ministry since his wife passed away.

The next deacon who responded to the survey was a local Byzantine (Ruthenian Rite) Catholic deacon. This deacon completed a two-year diaconal formation program at St. Gregory the Theologian Melkite Greek Catholic Seminary in 1996 and was ordained shortly thereafter. He considers himself a permanent deacon by calling and has served

Typika on numerous occasions in the Russian Catholic Center in San Francisco, where he was previously assigned, and in his present parish assignment. When he does so, he vests, censes and distributes Holy Communion but does not preach. This deacon does have occasion to teach the faith to others – in Eastern Catholic Fellowship, bible study and inquiry classes. He also takes the Holy Gifts to hospitals and shut-ins. He has his own spiritual father, other than his parish priest, and provides spiritual direction to others on a regular basis. He is an ex-officio member of his parish council but he does not receive compensation as a clergyman – even though he serves eight to nine services a week and assists with various administrative functions. This deacon has attended diocesan assemblies as a deacon and was recognized as a clergyman at those events. Other than this, the Eastern Catholic deacon did not have any comment to the open rhetorical questions posed.

The last deacon who responded was a Hierodeacon of the Independent Greek Orthodox Church. The Hierodeacon considers himself a permanent deacon due to his age (65) and his health. He served Typika on two occasions at his bishop's cathedral. When that occurred, he vested and censed. He does provide spiritual direction on a regular basis and has attended national/diocesan church conferences as a deacon with recognition as a clergyman. The Hierodeacon concludes that there is need for additional ministry in his context – "to distribute the Mysteries to the ill according to Orthodox tradition".

There were four laymen and four women who responded to the initial survey. In each case, one layman and one woman were Byzantine Catholic while the other three were OCA Christians. The first question asked if they knew of laymen and women being permitted to minister in various official capacities in the Eastern Churches. Interestingly, three men said they knew of this possibility while only one woman said she knew about it. Similarly, three men indicated that they have chanted a service for their communities in the absence of ordained clergy while only two women had done so. The ratio for visiting shut-ins and doing good works for needy members of the community is three out of four for both men and women. Only one layperson – a woman – indicated that she provides spiritual counseling to anyone on a regular basis. Three out of four women have either blessed their children or received the blessing of an elder layperson, while only two men have done so. Again, three out of four women think deacons should be ex-officio members of the parish council while only two men think so. With regard to whether deacons should receive compensation, the responses were minimal and qualified. For example, two men thought that they should be paid, however, one insisted that the deacon should be involved in weekly activities of the parish, and the other thought the compensation should be a stipend only and not a salary. Likewise, two women thought deacons should be paid, however, one thought that this should occur because his time spent in service may prevent him from being able to support his family. Regarding travel expenses being covered by the parish if he is a representative of the community, both three out of four men and women agreed that this should be done. Two laymen indicated that they had attended national conferences as delegates and one of them indicated that the parish covered his expenses. Unfortunately, no women polled indicated that she had attended conferences as a delegate of her parish. All eight men and women felt called by God to serve the church as lay people and all four men felt supported in exploring their ministry while only two women felt supported in exploring their ministries. Two out of four men and women both indicated that they feel affirmed in their ministries. Similarly, two men felt that their opinions are valued and supported while only one woman felt that this was the case. None of the laymen and women polled thought that there are any aspects of the ancient role of deacons that are no longer appropriate. In fact, one person commented that he feels that deacons in America need to be more than liturgical functionaries. Regarding the reinstitution of the female diaconate benefiting the church, two men and one woman thought it would. One man commented that it is spiritually and historically correct and another saw it as an expansion and development of women's ministries while one woman thought that a deaconess can assist with women being baptized and those who are ill. Finally, two men and two women indicated that there is a need for additional ministry in their churches. A parish council president (a man) indicated that the additional ministry in the church is most particularly needed from the laity. One woman offered an expanded commentary on this: "I see a lack of involvement in the church and a lack of desire to have more than just church by the majority of the people who go to church. Maybe I'm wrong, but it seems something is missing."

Before moving on to the gathering in Santa Fe, I will report the results of the follow up questionnaires.

Six out of thirteen attendees responded to the follow up survey. Among these respondents were my parish priest, one deacon, three laymen and two women. I will again start with my parish priest. My pastor didn't respond to the first question regarding what part of the conference stood out in his mind; however, he did think that active ministry does not only apply to the priesthood. Regarding the importance of *diaconia*, he equated it with Christianity and considers it of fundamental importance to all Christians. Regarding his needs being satisfied as a member of the community, he responded with questions of his own, but ultimately answered by saying, "our needs always exceed our satisfactions." Regarding whether he feels that he is serving the needs of others adequately, he responded that he "can always improve – as we all can." He felt that the wide variations of attendees contributed most positively to this conference. He stated that he gained no insights from the conference and that the conference did not change or increase his ministry at all. In this instance, and with subsequent responses that are ambivalent at best, this project admittedly failed to make an impression on this person. Even so, he stated that this type of conference could broaden the scope of understanding on a long-term basis; however, this conference did not have any personal effect on him. He stated that he would do it again, presumably because it could raise the consciousness of others. In response to the question about the restoration of the diaconate, my pastor stated that, "I was not aware that the ministry of the diaconate had been abandoned. There are few deacons who <u>will</u> or <u>can</u> devote themselves full-time to a specific ministry." Regarding the question of whether an expanded ministry of the diaconate and laity is traditional, my pastor responded with a question of his own; "What expanded ministry? We have always shared responsibility for ministry." In response to deacons strengthening Orthodox unity, he stated: "Every well trained Orthodox strengthens our faith and unity." Similarly, with respect to laymen and women working toward Orthodox unity and solving other problems he states: "Obviously, now how do we get them to classes?" My pastor indicated that he shared personal opinions about the conference with others, however, he did not comment on how these were received by those he spoke to. In response to the requested commentary on the restoration of diaconal ministry, he stated: "I wish my deacon had continued either of the two ministries he was given." And finally, he stated that, "active ministry is an integral part and natural result of my spiritual life as a priest."

The next respondent was a Hierodeacon of the Independent Greek Orthodox Church. The one thing that stood out in the mind of the Hierodeacon was "the importance of 'serving' and the importance that brings to worship." Moreover he feels that "serving is appropriate now, but it needs to be widened in scope." He feels that "inclusiveness and the presentations concerning all aspects of diaconia contributed positively to the conference and the single most valuable insight gained from the conference was "remembering the extent of my service as a deacon." Although this answer is vague, it reminds me of the phrase "May the Lord God remember thy diaconate in His Kingdom", which is significant as a formal means of recognition of the diaconate. His simple statement is similarly self-revelatory in that the conference apparently helped him become more aware of the many ways he can serve as a deacon. Thus, in this sense, his consciousness was raised. Regarding the restoration of diaconal ministry, he states: "Absolutely, it is needed and should be done because involvement is how we stay in God's grace." The Hierodeacon only comment on the restoration of diaconal ministry was to ask the question: "When will it happen?" Regarding the ministry of the laity, the Hierodeacon commented that, "it has happened in some circumstances already. Why not broaden the training and service of our laity?"

One male catechumen regarded *diaconia* as very important and said that "anytime deacons are serving the church or the wider community in Our Lord's name, it benefits all that come into contact with such service." Regarding the ministry of the laity, he stated that, "I would like to have an open forum for all to express themselves. Much the way this conference was presented." Yet another man (a former non-canonical Orthodox deacon) stated that the gathering on *diaconia* had a profound impact on his life noting that "I realized that the community I belonged to had no validity." His single most valuable insight as a result of attending this conference was to resolve to return to the Orthodox Church in America in order to receive legitimate sacraments. In short, this person felt that personal affiliation with other right-believing Christians is so important in his spiritual life that the very preservation of his soul depends on it. Yet another former clergyman who has found his niche as an Orthodox layman states that his single most valuable insight from this conference was "a reminder that the last judgment gospel (Matt. 25:31-46) sets our agenda for an active social ministry."

The commentary from the women was even more in depth as they responded to the follow up survey. My sense is that the following statements, as a whole, demonstrate how the project engaged them and made them think hard about the subject matter and its implications in our local context. One woman simply stated that she did not feel that her needs are being served adequately, stating, "I realize how busy and un-well Father is." She also feels that she would like "to see more opportunities to work together." Regarding the restoration of diaconal ministry, she states: "It helps meet the needs of the parishioners as well as the clergy." She then goes on to say simply, "it is needed." Regarding the ministry of the laity, she notes: "The more involved people become, the deeper their faith is." This woman concludes that active ministry "is an expression of my beliefs." The other woman polled stated that she was struck by "the lack of interest of the lay-people and the need for the church to have full-time deacons." Regarding whether things are all right the way they are, she responded that "it is not ok the way things are, because if things were the way they should be I believe the church would be stronger. God obviously has a design for the way He wants His church to be and we should do all we can to be within this design." This person later expanded on her thoughts in response to the question about the long-term effect that this type of conference might have on the church. She laments: "Ok, so I'm disappointed that few from our church came. So if we can't get the people to come then it obviously will have no effect. However, if the people had attended, I believe it could help the local church as well as the wider church in many ways. Increasing understanding should increase desire, which if acted upon would hopefully bring spiritual growth and change in people's lives and ultimately in the church as a whole." Responding to the question of how diaconal ministry would benefit the church, this person said; "Yes. Wouldn't restoring a broken bone in the hand make the hand function better, making the arm function better, making the body as a whole better and making the person better able to tend to the tasks at hand?" Regarding the ministry of the laity, this person said, "I think there seems to be a lack of it. People need to do more than just participate in fundraisers. But I don't know how the Orthodox Church views ministry by the laity when it comes to the spiritual things, like bible studies, etc." Finally, this woman had even more to offer in response to the question about the correlation between active ministry and the spiritual life. She states:

"I think it should have everything to do with your spiritual life. I think obviously you can fake it and be very active, but I think that if you are active in your relationship with God that your ministry is a natural overflow and a reflection of your inner life. Ultimately your ministry is pointless if you have no life in Christ, and though God can use it if He so choose, it most likely just brings more chaos than good in the long run. Christ is the head of the church and we should look to Him for direction. So it seems to me that if we are not abiding in Him, we are not really able to fulfill His purposes for our life and ministry. And if we have no life in Christ or "spiritual life", then we are unable to truly make an eternal difference. And isn't that the point of ministry, and the point of the church here on earth – to make an eternal difference? Isn't the point of all our good works that people should see them and glorify our Father in Heaven? Ministry is so much more than what we do physically, it is an outpouring of what we are doing spiritually, if we are in Christ."

Again, by way of analysis, the gathering in Albuquerque was significant for various reasons. Firstly, it represents the local context of my ministry. More importantly, it was significant because it moved one person to rejoin canonical Orthodoxy for the sake of his salvation and to enjoy the communion of the Eastern Orthodox Church throughout the world. This was the epitome of consciousness-raising, because he came to appreciate the diaconate enough to realize that he didn't really have it and decided to stop behaving as though he did.

In my case, there seems to be a discontinuity between what my parish priest believes about my ministry and what it actually is. That accounts for his responses about what his deacon is permitted to do. (Other deacons have served in my parish from time to time.) I have led Typika in his absence, completely vested, censing the church, chanting litanies and distributing Holy Communion with his knowledge and permission. I have preached one sermon that I composed myself; however, this was a requirement for the Homiletics course, which was a requirement of the Doctor of Ministry program, which in turn sparked this very project. However, all of this occurred prior to the suppression of these privileges by our bishop. Otherwise Fr. George granted a temporary exception to the expressed wishes of our bishop in response to the pastoral needs of our community during his extended vacation in Russia. Therefore, it is not indicative of a ministry that I could do whenever I so choose, having the blessing and approval of my bishop – as we have already seen and will see again shortly. Finally, I believe that the results of the gathering in Albuquerque definitely indicate the need for additional ministry.

E. Results of the Synaxis in Santa Fe:

As with the project colloquium in Pennsylvania and the gathering in Albuquerque, the first category of survey respondents to review is that of presbyters – especially since no bishops or monastics were present at the gathering in Santa Fe. The representational statistics for the *synaxis* in Santa Fe were as follows: two priests, one deacon, seven laymen and one woman. As with my report on the results of Albuquerque, particular emphasis will be given to the responses of the pastor of the host church as well as that of the resident deacon. Therefore, the first set of survey responses was from an Archpriest.

The Archpriest considers the diaconate to be both transitional and permanent because there are both in the church. He has allowed a deacon to serve Typika for his community over 24 times. When this occurs, the deacon vests and preaches his own sermons but does not cense. According to the Archpriest, the parish deacon does have an opportunity to formally teach the faith to others in adult education and nursing homes. Although his deacon does not have a spiritual father other than himself, the Archpriest stated that, "he could". The Archpriest also stated that his deacon would be permitted to provide spiritual direction to anyone on a regular basis, but he currently does not. His deacon is an ex-officio member of the parish council but the only compensation that the deacon can expect to receive is "heavenly treasure", according to the Archpriest. The deacon has not attended a national conference as a delegate in the Orthodox Church; however, he has attended diocesan assemblies but not as a clergy delegate. In response to the question about the number of services the deacon is expected to serve, the Archpriest stated; "he usually serves at four services." The Archpriest indicated that his deacon takes care of the administration of the parish and that he will continue to serve his community as usual in the future. The Archpriest stated that he does not feel that there are aspects of the ancient role of the diaconate that are no longer appropriate and went on to say that there is a need in his church for additional ministry in some form of lay diaconate.

The next priest to respond was the local Greek Orthodox priest and Economos – a formal title that roughly translates as 'steward'. The Economos feels that the diaconate is "transitional for those called to the priesthood and permanent for those called to the diaconate." Unfortunately, the Economos does not have a deacon in his parish, so he did not respond to the initial survey except to say that he does not feel that there are any aspects of the ancient role of the diaconate that are no longer appropriate.

The sole deacon present (other than myself) at this event was a venerable Archdeacon. The Archdeacon considers the diaconate to be vocational, rather than either transitional or permanent. He has served Typika for his community over 10 times. When doing so, he vests, censes and preaches his own sermons. He also distributes Holy Communion. According to him, he does not have occasion to formally teach the faith to others, but he has had occasion to baptize a person who was near death and he has taken the Holy Gifts to hospitals and shut-ins. The Archdeacon also provides spiritual direction to others on a regular basis. He is an ex-officio member of his parish council but he does not vote. Finally, he does not feel that there are any aspects of the ancient role of the diaconate that are no longer appropriate and he does not think there is any need for additional ministry in his ecclesiastical context.

Regarding the seven laymen who attended, six of them were aware that laymen and women are permitted to minister in various official capacities in the Orthodox Church prior to attending this gathering. Four of the seven said they had chanted a service for their community in the absence of ordained clergy and the same number said they had occasion to teach the faith to others. All seven men said they have either visited shut-ins or done good deeds for needy parishioners. One person indicated that he provides spiritual counseling to others regularly. Five men have either blessed their children or previously taken the blessing of an elder layman. Again, five men thought that deacons should be ex-officio members of the parish council. Four of the seven men thought that the parish deacon should be compensated, but all seven felt that deacons' travel expenses should be covered if they represent the parish. Only three out of seven men had ever attended a national or regional church conference as delegates and only one had his travel expenses covered by the church. Six out of seven men felt a calling to serve the church as laymen and all six felt supported and affirmed in their ministries. Again, all seven men felt that their opinions are valued and supported in the parish. Only one man thought that there are certain aspects of the ancient role of the diaconate that are no longer appropriate. His rationale was that the priest has properly taken to himself the role of baptism and confession – except for extreme need. Four out of seven men felt that the reinstitution of the order of deaconess would benefit the church and the same number of men felt a need for additional ministry in their parish. The men in Santa Fe offered quite a few interesting comments and suggestions. For example, one man thought that, "we need to emphasize to the laity that they have a mission and a function as members of the priesthood of God. All God's work is not just to be done by ordained ministers." Another suggestion was for "a paid assistant, whether ordained or not, for the pastor and the church." Along these lines, yet another man suggested that, "a diaconal team led by the priest and head deacon would be great." However, the same person followed that statement by saying that the need for "more time for discussion and actual community action plans would be great!"

The sole woman in Santa Fe was not aware that laymen and women were permitted to minister in various official capacities in the Orthodox Church. However, she had chanted a service for her community in the absence of ordained clergy on one previous occasion. She did not answer many parts of the survey because, as she said, "I don't feel like I've been in the church long enough to be qualified to answer these." Nevertheless, she indicated that she felt a calling to serve in the church as a layperson and also felt supported and affirmed in exploring and sustaining her ministry. Interestingly, regarding the reinstitution of the female diaconate, she states; "Perhaps by *economia* to support isolated women's monasteries, or parishes growing faster than new clergy. If it were extended to non-monastics, it seems to me that there wouldn't be a clear need if we clearly defined and supported the lay ministry roles of women." Regarding the need for additional ministry in her parish, she stated; "I do feel that there should be more focus on the lay ministry as a calling of all the people – that the people are not the subjects of ministry, but rather Christ primarily and secondarily to one another through Him."

Out of eleven participants at the Santa Fe *Synaxis*, six people responded to the follow-up questionnaire. Of these respondents, there were two priests, one deacon and three laymen. Again, since the respondents are identifiable, I found it interesting to note the differences in perspectives from priests, to those of the deacons to those of the laity.

The Archpriest mentioned that the good discussion and brotherly spirit were the characteristics that stood out in his mind about the gathering. He also felt that *diaconia* applies to all Christians. He noted that *diaconia* is very important and we need ongoing reminders about what it means to serve. In response to the question about his needs (as a human being and a member of the community) being served, the Archpriest said: "The question is: Is the Lord being served adequately?" The Archpriest thought that "praying first, then talking and eating together in a relaxed setting" contributed most positively to the conference. The single most important insight gained from the conference was the fact "that in some churches the diaconate is not functioning as fully as I am used to." With regard to change in ministry after the conference, the Archpriest stated; "I don't think there have been many changes, but some of our laity are more interested in the ordained diaconate." The Archpriest thought that "a fuller expression of the diaconate – both ordained and lay", might have a long-term effect on the church. He went on to offer a specific personal reflection, stating that "it has produced a greater desire to see the ministry of service lived out by every member of the church." He also considered the event worthwhile in general. Regarding the restored diaconal ministry benefiting the church, the Archpriest stated: "The deacons who have served in our church seem to be living out a fully restored diaconate, and it has definitely helped. I hope every church can experience the same level of commitment and ministry." The Archpriest absolutely feels that an expanded ministry of the laity and diaconate is faithful to tradition and that well-trained deacons and laymen can serve to bring about and strengthen Orthodox unity. The Archpriest shared information about the conference with others and indicated that the information was well received. Commenting on the restoration of diaconal ministry, the Archpriest stated, "most of the deacons I know are living a very full 'restored' diaconate." Commenting on the expanded role of the laity, he said, "the role of the laity is to minister whatever gifts have been given to them by the Holy Spirit, for the building up of the body." Finally, the Archpriest believes that "each person has been given talents and will be judged on how they used them to the glory of God."

The Economos thought that the fellowship and exchange among participants stood out the most in his mind. He does not think that *diaconia* applies only to the priesthood, rather he thinks that "all members of the church should fulfill their assigned role." He feels that his needs are being served adequately and he is serving the needs of others adequately and found that the presentations by the priests contributed most positively to the conference. According to the Economos, the single most valuable insight that he gained from the conference was that "I didn't understand the purpose of the conference", i.e., that he was not aware of any problem in the contemporary diaconate. This is ironic because he seems to be the only one who didn't understand the purpose of the conference and it is unfortunate because this indicates a certain failure of the project to raise his consciousness vis-a-vis the diaconate. He then went on to indicate that the conference had no effect on him or his ministry nor did he sense that it would have any long-term effect on the church. In fact, he stated that he didn't think it was worth his time and he would not do it again. The Economos stated, "the diaconate has not been abolished so it need not be restored." He also feels that "the training of deacons has nothing to do with Orthodox unity." However, he did note, "every member of the church, clergy and laity should be well-learned in the tradition of the church. Much of Her problems are the result of misunderstanding." Finally, the Economos stated, "the laity has a ministerial role that it is not fully performing. Until it fulfills its current role, we should not talk about expanding it."

The Archdeacon thought that the use of scripture to support the diaconate, and two priests attending and participating stood out in his mind as the most important aspects of the conference. He stated, "*diaconia* applies to all Christians – lay and ordained. Each can set an example to the other." Interestingly, the Archdeacon states: "I am not concerned with *diaconia*. However, *diaconia* is important, and the proof of this is seen from statements made by Metropolitan PHILIP in that he wants a deacon to serve in every parish." The Archdeacon feels that his needs are satisfied very adequately, but he regrets that he "will never feel completely adequate in serving the needs of others in our community. As I am getting older, I am frustrated that I cannot do more." For the Archdeacon, "the factors that contributed positively to our conference in Santa Fe were the participation of two priests, and the attendance of several lay members. All were there to support the diaconate and feel that the ordained deacons are a vital part of the church worship and outreach." His single most valuable insight gained from the conference is "that there is great interest in the ordained diaconate." According to the Archdeacon, "the conference did not change my ministry but strengthened my outlook that more service to Christ is needed in our community." The Archdeacon went on to say "who knows what long term effect such conferences do have. They certainly help the church." Thus, the Archdeacon indicated that the conference had no personal effect on him; however, he noted that it was worth his time and he would do it again. He went on to say, "diaconal ministry is important to the church and will meet the growing needs of the Orthodox in America. There are never enough servants for the Lord. The need is great." He also said, "expanded ministry of the laity and diaconate is faithful to tradition and well-trained deacons will strengthen Orthodox unity. In their work in the community, they can say to the un-churched 'just come and see'." Likewise, he noted that, "well-informed laymen and women who know the love of Christ can resolve any problems common to Orthodox in America, or to non-Orthodox, or to non-Christians." Finally, the Archdeacon stated: "I am sorry. I did not know the ministry of the diaconate needed restoration. I thought the ministry was alive and well."

Since all of the responses of the lay-participants in Santa Fe were narratives, I will simply proceed with their statements as follows. One person said:

"I didn't find anything in the conference that really stood out in my mind. I believe that we are all called to ministry, but as St. Paul says, 'we have different gifts'. I feel that *diaconia* is important and serves an important role in our community. It probably varies from community to community, but could be as vibrant or as conservative as the deacons make it. I feel that my needs are being met at church, and I feel that I am reaching out to others working with the homeless and shut-ins. I didn't gather any new insights from the conference or feel that it has changed my ministry or increased my service to Christ in my community. I continue to do what I was doing prior to the conference. I apologize if I missed something, but I don't see any long-term impact for me from the conference. Perhaps it would be more beneficial for those not actively involved in ministry."

Another person was impressed by how much the diaconate encompasses. Moreover, he stated: "*Diaconia* is important and a concerted effort should be made to recruit new deacons and lay ministers. My needs are being served and I am increasing in the service to others." He proceeded by stating: "The active participation of the conference members contributed positively to the conference and the single most valuable insight that I gained from the conference was that I can provide service in any way I am able. This conference has made me expand my thinking of what service can be. The long-term effect is that if more people really understand what is proffered, the church could start seeing more people stepping forward to the diaconate and other clerical vocations. This conference reinforced my inclination to serve. It was worth my time and I would do it again. I think the restoration of the diaconate will provide much needed help to our overworked and overburdened bishops and priests. I think that expanded ministry is traditional and it is a good bet that deacons and laymen and women can bring about Orthodox unity and resolve other problems that we face in America. The expanded role of the laity is what I believe the early church encouraged, as did Christ and active ministry provides direction, instruction and support, as well as a refuge from the world when it becomes overwhelming."

The third and final laymen commented in a similar manner, although even more extensively:

> "Q&A Discussion of the steps towards the ordained diaconate and the role of music/chant as well as the importance of the laity – the 'royal priesthood' – stand out in my mind. *Diaconia* doesn't only apply to the ordained priesthood. There is cause for concern about *diaconia*. For example, my needs are being served but I am not serving the needs of others adequately. Regarding the conference, the open format was conducive to reflection on how the particular interests

and the circumstances of those present contributed positively to the conference – one size does not fit all."

This same person continued by saying:

"The single most valuable insight that I had from the conference was that *Diaconia* is an organic outgrowth of the needs of the church as it is present in any particular community. No specific contribution can be singled out regarding the personal effect this conference has had on me. Rather, it is part of an ongoing personal exploration in conjunction with my spiritual father regarding my service to the church. Conferences like this, if widespread, may have a positive impact on one's motivation and ability to serve the church, moving him beyond just considering the options on to action. I don't necessarily agree with the premise that the diaconate is in need of 'restoration', having always had a very positive experience of vital deacons within parishes. However, there is always room for improvement and a more active diaconate on the whole would, among many other goods, relieve pressure from priests and parish council committees to serve all the needs of the congregation. I have summarized this experience with my wife and have continued to encourage others to move from idea to action regarding their own service to the church. The expanded ministerial role of the laity is crucial to the living vitality of the church, as Abbot Jonah Paffhausen has said. There is in Orthodoxy no 'salvation by association'. We cannot hope to be saved merely by going to church, we cannot leave the spiritual work of the church to the ordained clergy alone. We are the church. We are the Body of Christ and inheritors of his power. And to quote Spider-man: 'with great power comes great responsibility'. So what does active ministry have to do with my life? At the heart of our faith is sacrificial love of neighbor. I will not become alive spiritually without service to others, without giving of myself to attend to their needs. The greatest of needs is the need for Christ. I and all Christians are therefore required to manifest Christ for others – this is the meaning of ministry to me."

From this analysis of the gathering in Santa Fe, we can conclude from the results that the gathering was very significant. By contrast to the gathering in Albuquerque, the situation was vastly different – even though the two churches are only 60 miles away from one another and the territory of the Diocese of Mid-America and the Diocese of the South overlap and the two bishops are close friends. I firmly believe that the responses from the Archpriest, Archdeacon and parishioners of Holy Trinity Orthodox Church indicate that the diaconate is alive and well in this ecclesiastical context. Two statements by the priest and deacon in their follow-up surveys demonstrate this best. The Archpriest stated essentially that he is aware that the diaconate elsewhere is not functioning as fully as it is in his own parish. That accounts for the consistent rejection of the notion that the diaconate is in need of restoration – especially by the Archdeacon himself. In this case, the diaconate is obviously not in need of restoration.

F. Evaluation of Project Data:

At this point, in this presentation, I want to restate the problem arising out of my ministry as a deacon in a mission parish of the Diocese of the South (Orthodox Church of America) in stark and no-uncertain terms. That way, I can analyze the project results in terms of how they relate to the issues I face as a deacon. I can think of no better way to do this than to first respond to my own questionnaires and then see how that data compares to the data collected from the project.

The national church I serve in is the Orthodox Church in America. The Mission Statement adopted by the Holy Synod of Bishops of the

OCA in 1990 says, among other things, that it is "to be the body of Christ in North America and to be faithful to the tradition of the Holy Orthodox Church." We have already seen how the data rendered through this research project overwhelmingly demonstrates that an expanded ministry of the diaconate is faithful to tradition. Likewise, the mission statement that was adopted by my mission parish on August 8, 2002 also recognizes All Saints of North America Orthodox Church as being faithful to tradition under the authority of the Diocese of the South and the Orthodox Church in America. However, it also pledges a commitment to practicing the spiritual life through various forms of ministry, all of which culminate in *diaconia*: "We are committed to living Orthodox Christian spiritual lives, struggling to keep God's commandments through liturgical and sacramental worship, prayer, education, witness, fellowship, stewardship and service." Unfortunately, as we have seen from participants at the *synaxis* in Albuquerque, there is need for additional ministry in this entire ecclesiastical context. I am quite sure that there are qualified clergy and laity, whether deacons, subdeacons, readers, monastics or laymen and women who can rise to meet this need if given the chance and encouraged to do so. However, some things like distributing Holy Communion in Typika or taking the Holy Gifts to the sick, elderly and infirm should only be done by deacons who have been given permission to do so by their bishops and with the knowledge and blessing of their priests. This is certainly not the case in my circumstances. I am not allowed to lead a Typika service vested because there is no priest to bless the vestments. If I were to lead Typika (Typical Psalms or a 'type' of liturgy), I could not cense because there is no priest to bless the censer, nor am I supposed to chant litanies because there is no priest present to conclude them with an *ecphonesis* prayer. Likewise, I am not able to preach my own sermons. Rather, I can only read a homily that has been composed by a priest with the blessing of my parish priest. In nearly five years I have been able to do this only two or three times. In my parish, the only one who has occasion to teach the Orthodox faith to adults is the parish priest. I did get involved with our church school once but was asked by the parish priest not to interfere with the lessons given by the other church school teachers, so I no longer have an opportunity to teach the faith to others in a formal setting. When I have been blessed to serve my community in the absence of the priest, I do so as a volunteer as there is no line item in the parish budget for deacons and the auxiliary clergy fund is used for our bishop and supply priests. In addition, I am not permitted to serve as an ex-officio member of the parish council. Even my wife is deemed ineligible for election, so I am completely out of touch with parish business except indirectly as I provide professional insurance services to the parish. I once attended the All-American Council of the Orthodox Church in America, as a delegate. However, I was considered a lay-delegate, even though I was taking care of a mission that had no priest at the time and could have been designated a clergy representative if my pastor had consented along with the council representative of the priestless mission. Neither mission had anything to lose and everything to gain, since my wife attended as an alternate lay-delegate and I would have provided the priestless mission with a clergy delegate – thus giving the New Mexico delegation four votes instead of three. But since my parish priest declined my request during registration, the case was closed. Ironically, I have attended diocesan assemblies and deanery meetings as a clergyman; however, my parish did not reimburse my travel expenses, as they were when I attended the national church council as a lay-delegate. In brief, my ministry has been limited to a liturgical function in my ecclesiastical context. Now I will review and compare this situation with the combined results of the project as a whole to see if any possible solution to the problem can be drawn from this.

Out of twelve total upper echelon clerics, consisting of eleven priests and one bishop, ninety-two percent allow deacons to serve Typika for their communities. Of these, ninety-two percent allow the deacons to vest for Typika, seventy-five percent allow the deacons to cense and to preach, and fifty-eight percent allow the deacons to distribute Holy Communion. Eighty-three percent of the upper two ranks of the clerical hierarchy provide their deacons with opportunities to teach the faith to others in a formal setting. Seventy-five percent allow the deacons to take the Holy Gifts to hospitals and shut-ins and fifty-eight percent permit the deacons in their charge to provide spiritual direction to others on a regular basis. Forty-two percent of the deacons are ex-officio members of their parish councils and only thirty-three percent are compensated for their labors. From this we can conclude it is possible for a deacon such as myself to provide a great measure of pastoral ministry. However, we have only a one in three chance to expect compensation for our support services, but a somewhat better chance to sit on a governing board to oversee parish business.

Out of thirty-eight deacons and diaconal candidates, fifty-five percent are allowed to serve Typika for their communities. Of these, thirty-seven percent do so vested, thirty-four percent cense, forty percent preach (half of whom compose their own sermons), and twenty-six percent distribute Holy Communion. Fifty-eight percent of deacons and diaconal candidates polled have occasion to teach the faith to others formally. Eighteen percent are allowed to take the Holy Gifts to hospitals and shut-ins. Twenty-one percent regularly provide spiritual direction to others. Twenty-six percent of those polled serve as ex-officio members of their parish councils and forty percent of these vote while the remainder function as advisory members. Only eleven percent of deacons are compensated for the time and effort they spent providing service for their communities. Keeping in mind that sixty-one percent of those polled were diaconal candidates, we can attribute these relatively low percentiles to the fact that there is a huge discrepancy over the perception of diaconal candidates and purely ceremonial deacons, compared to priests, bishops and deacons with parish or institutional ministry experience. Another possibility is that many respondents in this category are laymen and that the statistical results of the survey reflect this fact. I generally suspect a combination of these two possibilities because there is a big difference in the results of this category of respondents with regard to this question as compared to the priests and bishops. Nevertheless, the responses are nevertheless relative to those of the priests and prelates with only two exceptions - teaching and communion. For example, the percentile for teaching spiked because many diaconal candidates have opportunity to teach the faith in church school and other venues, as do deacons. Conversely, the percentiles for taking the Holy Gifts and distributing Holy Communion dipped or remained relatively consistent with the ratios given by the priests because deacons distinctly do those activities. Even so, the results are still significant because more than half of the deacons and diaconal candidates perform Typika in the absence of a priest and most of them provide priestly functions. Thus, we can conclude that deacons are more than mere Lectors or Acolytes, as the scope of their duties demonstrates. However, the reality is that they generally do not cast votes in parish business or directly influence policy matters, neither do the majority of deacons get paid for what they actually do for their parishes.

Out of thirty-eight laymen and women who participated in this project, fifty-eight percent knew that laymen and women are permitted to minister in various official capacities in the Orthodox Church. Twenty-six percent have chanted services for their communities in the absence of ordained clergy. Fifty-eight percent teach the faith to others in a formal capacity. Thirty-four percent have visited shut-ins or done good works for needy members of their communities on their own accord. Five percent of the laity provide spiritual counseling to others on a regular basis. Twenty-six percent have either blessed younger people or received the blessing of elder laypersons. Sixty-six percent of the laity feel that deacons should be ex-officio members of their parish councils. Forty-two percent of the laity feel that deacons should be compensated for their efforts in the parishes, but eighty-two percent feel that the parish should reimburse deacons for travel expenses incurred when they attend regional or national conferences as representatives of their parishes. Eighty-seven percent of those polled felt a calling to serve their communities as lay-ministers. Sixty-eight percent feel supported in the exploration of their ministries and the same number felt that their opinions are valued and supported. Seventy-six percent felt affirmed in the ministries that they are actually performing. Only three percent felt that the ancient role of the diaconate is no longer appropriate. Fifty-five percent felt that the reinstitution of the office of deaconess would benefit the church. Finally, thirty-four percent felt that additional ministry is necessary in their churches. From these results, we can conclude that most laymen and women feel called to minister as laymen and women.

Most of them also feel affirmed and supported in their ministries. Regarding the diaconate, the vast majority would probably not object to their parishes reimbursing deacons for travel expenses they incur for representing the parish at conferences and they also generally think that deacons should be ex-officio members of the parish council. However, the results seem to indicate that the laity would likely object to deacons receiving compensation from the parish due to their status in the parish. I suspect that this may vary based upon church finances and the scope of duties that the deacon is called upon to do for the parish.

With regard to the follow-up questionnaires, thirteen people responded. Interestingly, one hundred percent of the respondents thought that the concept of ministry is not limited to the ordained priesthood. Only fifteen percent felt that things are as they should be with regard to the importance of and need for *diaconia* in their parish circumstances. Sixty-nine percent thought that the restoration of the ancient ministry of the diaconate would benefit the church today. Sixty-two percent thought that the expanded ministry of the diaconate and laity is traditional. Eighty-five percent felt that well-trained deacons could serve to strengthen Orthodox unity and ninety-two percent felt that well-informed laity could resolve problems and foster Orthodox unity in America. The response indicates that the needs of the faithful are not being met adequately and that there is need for additional ministry from deacons and laymen and women. From this we can conclude that the status quo is unacceptable and the church should do everything possible to train its deacons and inform its laity about various opportunities for ministry in the Orthodox Church. Perhaps this will spark new life and enthusiasm into the Orthodox in North America and the church hierarchy will take notice and respond in kind with an optimistic, courageous and energetic renewal of their own – administrative unity.

G. Summary and Conclusion:

The big question is whether or not the goals and objectives of these conferences were achieved. I shall now review the goals and objected stated in the project proposal to discern an answer. One objective stated in my project proposal is to compare the present state of the diaconate in my own parish, diocese, national church and the wider church in North America with the wider responsibilities it might take on, thanks to the issues discussed in this project. I believe I have done that; however, I would add that I have also done this with *diaconia* in general. That is to say that the results of this project bear out the fact that there is a need for additional ministry for deacons in the Orthodox Church in North America. However, this is also true for all in the church, be they bishops, priests or laymen and women.

Another objective stated in my project proposal is that the surveys would do more than simply improve the content and format of this type of conference. Rather, they were intended to be learning devices that challenge the participants to put the information to good use. I used many open-ended questions for that very purpose and I firmly believe that the narrative responses that I have quoted in this paper clearly demonstrate that this objective was achieved. Moreover, the fifty-five and a half percent response from the follow-up questionnaires seem to indicate that the project made a lasting impression upon those who responded.

One long-term goal that has yet to be achieved is the restoration of the traditional scope of ministry of the diaconate to the contemporary church throughout North America. As mentioned previously, this can be achieved by continuing this program on a national scale in the future. I certainly hope that I am blessed to be a part of the continuation of this project in the future and that the Standing Conference of Canonical Orthodox Bishops in the Americas responds affirmatively to my request to sponsor such a Pan-Orthodox series of conferences. The proposed production of a series of instructional videos would achieve yet another goal of this project – the improvement of liturgical skills. This could lead to a far more important achievement – the eventual unity of Orthodox envisioned and prescribed by the canons and ecclesiology of the Orthodox Church.

Finally, this paper has allowed me to reflect upon how the project has changed my own understanding and practice of the diaconate and its ministry. Had it not been for the Doctor of Ministry program. I would not have been challenged to think critically about the ministry of the diaconate, let alone my personal ministry as a deacon.

This research has enabled me to define and analyze complex situations pertaining to ministry in general, and my ministry in particular. The process also identified various opportunities for service – not only for deacons, but also for this deacon. This learning process has allowed me to delve into the biblical and theological resources of the church in order to understand and deeply appreciate the great and awesome gift that God has bestowed upon me.

The research has helped me to distinguish between what the diaconate is and what it is not. It is a Holy Order, not an office that is held temporarily like the term of an elected member of a parish council. Here again, ordination in the Orthodox understanding has more than mere temporal significance – it has eschatological decisiveness and character. Sadly, this temporal office is what the diaconate has become in some denominations. In the Orthodox Church, it is one of the three degrees of priesthood, and is critically important in the life of the church, as Metropolitan Hierotheos explained: "Thus the work of the deacons, priests and bishops is connected with the spiritual growth of the Christians. According to the baptismal service as presented by St. Dionysios – and we believe that he is reflecting the usage in the first centuries of the church – when a person is brought for baptism, the deacons divest him of his garments; this shows their role in the Church as purifying. The priests anoint the candidate's whole body; this shows their role in the Church as illuminators. The bishops bring the candidate to perfection by baptizing him; this shows their perfecting role."

I take my role and identity as a deacon very seriously. In fact, I consider this project and paper as one way to fulfill my role as purifier, because this process has been a purification of sorts. That is, through considerable research and through the evaluation of a variety of perspectives, it is hoped that a deeper grasp of the truth has come from this project. This is not an academic work for its own sake, rather, it is an integration of the practice of ministry and academic work which has resulted in a greater appreciation of the diaconate. This learning and purification process is rather difficult. It is not easy for me to articulate a problem that I could turn a blind eye to, and I am quite sure it is not easy for others to take criticism from a deacon. After all, the purgative process of facing up to problems can be a painful ordeal for everyone and there is potential for conflict, alienation and compounded confusion over this process if not approached openly, honestly and with good will and humility. As I have learned from an elective independent study on conflict resolution as a part of this program, a full disclosure of the facts along with an open, honest and balanced dialogue can lead to a fruitful negotiation among rational people with differences. Thus, if anyone has taken offense at this full disclosure and examination of the facts and issues relating to priestly, diaconal and lay ministry, or the lack thereof in our ecclesiastical context, I humbly and sincerely apologize and ask forgiveness.

I hope that the fruit of this research project and paper will ultimately be the complete restoration of the diaconate. Am I effectively saying that all deacons should do all of the things that I have identified in this dissertation? Certainly not. As at least one respondent correctly points out that the scope of service depends upon the gifts that each individual deacon is blessed with. In my case, that means that those whom I trust and respect as co-laborers would recognize me as a trusted and respected brother and fellow minister in the vineyard of the Lord. This can manifest itself in various ways as exemplified by the project responses and the evidence presented in this paper for such things. For example, based upon the example from deacons in other jurisdictions as well as other parishes in the Diocese of the South, all previous banns with regard to Typika/Obednitza, including vesting, censing, preaching, litanies and the distribution of Holy Communion could be lifted. Furthermore, if I were to fill-in for the parish priest in any capacity (e.g., to teach a class or to lead a service), I should be given a special stipend for my time and efforts because it is simply the right thing to do. Likewise, I should be permitted to sit on the parish council as an ex-officio member with full voting privileges and be reimbursed for attending national or regional conferences as a church representative. Most importantly, I should be entrusted by the bishop to take the Holy

Gifts to the hospitalized or homebound faithful under the supervision of the parish priest.

There is still much to learn, so that the process, which this project has initiated, can and should continue. Thus, the continuation of this project with the blessing of my bishop and the endorsement of the Standing Conference of Canonical Orthodox Bishops in the Americas is my plan, hope and prayer for the future. In the meantime, I am going to take the advice of my spiritual father and wait upon the Will of God while not pushing my own will about my service as a deacon. I will remain active at the Holy Table. Lastly, hear this excellent encouragement given to discouraged deacons by Gary Straub and James Trader II in conclusion:

> "When seas are high and things get bad and you are thinking seriously of bailing out on your deaconing work, I invite you to keep in mind four ways that deacons can contribute to a solution. The first way is to keep our lives focused and centered on Christ. We do this by actually practicing our faith. We practice our faith by practicing the basic spiritual disciplines. No substitute exists for daily scripture meditation, singing our faith, Sabbath rest, living out God's forgiving and reconciling power, hospitality, intercession and generosity."

The End and Glory to God!

APPENDIX I

"THE DIACONATE IN CHRIST – Part I"

**A colloquium on the holy diaconate in conjunction with
the Antiochian House of Studies Residency Program
General Assembly Panelists:
Bishop THOMAS of Oakland, PA
Fr. Shalhoub, Fr. Allen, Fr. Najim, Fr. Viscuso, Fr. Bitar
Tuesday August 30, 2005
Agenda:**

1. Opening Prayer - Bishop Thomas.
2. Doctor of Ministry Survey on the Diaconate – Deacon David Mascarenas.
3. Brief stories about students' paths to Orthodoxy.
4. Orthodoxy in South Africa – Fr. Athinodoros Papaevripiades.
5. Orthodoxy in Ireland – Fr. Irenaeus DuPlessis.
6. Contemporary Questions:
    A. What is the most pressing issue facing Orthodoxy in America today? Will we see the unification of Orthodox jurisdictions under one ecclesial administration in our lifetime?
    B. What is your opinion with regard to producing one Standard English translation of the service of the Church for use by all the Churches involved in SCOBA?
    C. Other questions from the floor.

APPENDIX IA

"DIACONIA IN NEW MEXICO"

Seminar on the ministry of priests, deacons
and laity in the Orthodox Church

Sponsored by the New Mexico Orthodox Clergy Association
Panelists:
The Very Reverend George Sondergaard, Rev. Fr.
Mario Giannopoulos, Rev. Gabriel Bulz,
Rev. Deacon David Mascarenas, Rev. Deacon George Collaros

Saturday, September 10, 2005
All Saints of North America Orthodox Church
Albuquerque, NM

9:30 – 10:30 AM	Matins
10:30 – 10:45 AM	Introduction of Panelists and Participants.
10:45 – 11:00 AM	Presentation by Archpriest George Sondergaard: *The Son of Man came not to be ministered unto, but to minister, and to give his life as a ransom for many.*
11:00 – 11:15 AM	Open Discussion "On Priestly *Diaconia*"
11:15 – 11:30 AM	Presentation by Deacon David Mascarenas: *The Ministry of the Diaconate in the Orthodox Church*
11:30 – 11:45 AM	Open Discussion "On the *Diaconate* in Christ"

11:45 –Noon	Presentation by Rev. Fr. Mario Giannopoulos: *"The Laborer is Worthy of His Wages - Axios!"*
Noon– 12:15 PM	Open Discussion *"On the priestly office of every Orthodox Christian and the ministry of the laity in the Orthodox Church"*
12:15 - ?	Luncheon

Seminar Registration

Name _____

Address _____

City _____ State/Prov. _____

Zip/Postal Code _____

Home Phone _____

Work Phone _____

Parish, Community or Institution: _____

Diocese: _____

Priest: _____ Deacon: _____ Subdeacon: _____

Lector/Altar Server: _____ Layperson: _____

Clergy should bring a set of vestments and be prepared to serve.

Suggested Donation: $10.00 (Includes Lunch). *Please send check or money order payable to*: All Saints of North America Orthodox Church 10440 4th Street NW, Albuquerque, NM 87114. For more information contact Archpriest George Sondergaard at 505/271-1515 or Deacon David Mascarenas at 505/833-5454.

APPEΝΟΙΧ ΙΒ

"DIACONIA IN NEW MEXICO"

Seminar on the ministry of priests, deacons
and laity in the Orthodox Church

Sponsored by the New Mexico Orthodox Clergy Association
Panelists:
Rev. Fr. John Bethancourt, Rev. Fr. Demetrios
Demopoulos, Rev. Gabriel Bulz,
Rev. Deacon David Mascarenas, Rev. Deacon Basil Reeves.

October 15, 2005
Holy Trinity Orthodox Church
Santa Fe, NM

Saturday, October 15, 2005

9:30 – 10:30 AM	*Orthros*
10:30 – 10:45 AM	Introduction of Panelists and Participants.
10:45 – 11:00 AM	Presentation by Fr. John Bethancourt: *The Son of Man came not to be ministered unto, but to minister, and to give his life as a ransom for many.*
11:00 – 11:15 AM	Open Discussion "On Priestly *Diaconia*"
11:15 – 11:30 AM	Presentation by Deacon David Mascarenas: *The Ministry of the Diaconate in the Orthodox Church*

11:30 – 11:45 AM	Open Discussion "On the *Diaconate* in Christ
11:45 – Noon	Presentation by Rev. Fr. Demetrios Demopoulos: *"The Laborer is Worthy of His Wages - Axios!"*
Noon – 12:15 PM	Open Discussion *"On the priestly office of every Orthodox Christian and the ministry of the laity in the Orthodox Church"*
12:15 - ?	Luncheon

Seminar Registration

Name _____

Address _____

City _____ State/Prov. _____ Zip/
Postal Code _____

Home Phone _____

Work Phone _____

Parish, Community or Institution: _____

Diocese: _____

Priest: ____ Deacon: ____ Subdeacon: ____ Lector/Altar Server: ____
Layperson: ____
Clergy should bring a set of vestments and be prepared to serve.

Suggested Donation: $10.00 (Includes Lunch). Please send check or money order payable to Holy Trinity Orthodox Church, 231 E. Cordova Rd., Santa Fe, NM 87501 For more information contact Fr. John Bethancourt at 505/983-5821 or Deacon David Mascarenas at 505/833-5454.

APPENDIX IIA

Participant Survey for Laymen and Women

What is your age? _____ What is your gender? _____ Your Diocese? _____

Are you a convert to the Orthodox Church? _____ Previous faith, if so _____

Are you a Parish Councilor? _____ If not, were you a parish councilor? _____

Do you serve on any committees or hold any specialized function or office? _____
If so, what?

Have you ever affiliated with any other Orthodox jurisdictions? _____ Which?

Have you considered, or are you considering a clerical or monastic vocation? ____

Is your church context a Mission? _____ Parish? _____ Monastery? _____ Other?

Were you ever ordained? _____ If so, when and to what? _____

Are you married? _____ Do you have any children? _____ How many? _____

Highest level of education: Grade School ___ College ___ Graduate School ___

Are you a seminary graduate? _____ Seminary_____ Graduation year _____

Are you familiar with the Antiochian House of Studies or similar certification programs?

Did you know that laymen and women are permitted to minister in various official capacities in the Orthodox Church prior to attending this conference? _____

Have you ever chanted a service for your community in the absence of ordained clergy? _____ Number of Occasions _____

Do you have occasion to formally teach the faith to others? _____ If so, on what occasion?

Have you ever baptized anyone personally? _____ If so, under what circumstances?

Have you ever visited shut-ins or done favors for needy members of the community? ___

Do you have a spiritual father other than your parish priest? _____

Does your spouse, if married? _____ Do your children, if any? _____

Do you provide spiritual counseling to anyone on a regular basis? _____

Have you ever blessed your children or grandchildren or received the blessing of an elder layperson?

Do you think a deacon should be an ex-officio member of your parish council?

Do you think Subdeacons should be eligible to be elected to serve on the parish council?

Are clergy family members eligible to be elected to your parish council? _____ Should they be eligible?

Does your deacon receive any compensation as a clergyman? _____ Should he? Why/Why not?

Should the parish cover national or regional church conference travel expenses for a deacon if he is a clergy representative of your community? _____ Why/Why not?

Have you ever attended a national or regional church conference as a lay delegate? _____

Did the parish cover your travel expenses? _____

What is your profession/ occupation? _____

How many services do you attend on a weekly basis? _____

Do you feel called by God to serve in the Church as a layperson?

If so, do you feel supported in exploring your ministry?

If not, do you feel exploited or pressured by church officials to serve against your will?

How do you serve the Church in your context? Please describe:

Do you feel affirmed in your ministry?

Do you feel that your opinion is valued and supported in your parish?

Are there any aspects of the ancient role of deacons that you feel are no longer appropriate? If so, which aspects (please state the reason you feel this is so):

Do you think that the reinstitution of the Order of Deaconess would benefit the Church? If so, why or why not?

Do you feel that there is a need for additional ministry in your ecclesiastical context?

Please explain and offer suggestions for improvement and any additional information on the reverse.

APPENDIX iiB

Participant Survey for Deacons and Diaconal Candidates

What jurisdiction do you serve in?

_____

Are you a convert to the Orthodox Church? _____ Previous faith,
if so _____

Are you a Deacon, Subdeacon, Reader or
Layman? _____

If deacon, have you served in any other Orthodox jurisdictions?
_____ Which?

If you are an Altar-Server, Reader or Subdeacon, are you training to
become a Deacon?:

Do you serve in a Mission? _____ Parish? _____ Monastery? _____
Other? _____

When were you ordained to the diaconate? _____ What
is your age? _____

Are you married? _____ Do you have any children? _____
How many? _____

Highest level of education: Grade School _____ College _____ Graduate School _____

Are you a seminary graduate? _____ Seminary_____ Graduation year _____

Did you go through the House of Studies or similar program? _____ Completion date:

Do you consider yourself as a transitional, permanent deacon or neither? _____

Why? _____ _____

Have you ever served Typika for your community? _____ Number of Occasions _____

If so, do you vest? _____ If so, do you cense? _____ If so, do you preach? _____ If so, do you compose your sermons? _____ If so, do you distribute Holy Communion? _____

If not, do you lead Vespers w/o a priest or Reader Svs? _____ If so, with litanies? _____

Have you preached on any other occasions? _____ If so, when? _____

Do you have occasion to formally teach the faith to others? _____ If so, on what occasion?_____ _____

Have you ever baptized anyone personally? _____ If so, under what circumstances?

Have you taken the Holy Gifts to hospitals? _____ Shut-ins? _____
Other? _____

Do you have a spiritual father other than your parish priest? _____

Does your wife, if married? _____ Do your children, if any? _____

Do you provide spiritual direction to anyone on a regular
basis? _____

Have you ever blessed a religious article or other object? _____ If so,
what? _____

Are you an ex-officio member of your parish council as a deacon?
_____ Do you vote?:

If a Subdeacon, are you eligible to be elected to serve on the parish
council? _____

Are your family members eligible to be elected to the parish
council? _____

Do you receive any compensation as a clergyman? _____ If so,
what? _____

Have you ever attended a National Church Conference as a delegate
as a Deacon? _____

If so, where you a clergy-delegate or a lay-
delegate? _____

Have you attended Diocesan Assemblies as a Deacon? _____

Are you considered a clergy delegate at such events? _____

What is your profession/occupation?_____
_____

How many services do you serve on a weekly basis? _____

Are there any aspects of the traditional role of the diaconate
that you do that are not mentioned above? If so, please
describe: _____

Are there any aspects of the ancient role of the diaconate that you feel
are no longer appropriate? If so, which aspects (please state the reason
you feel this is so): _____

How will this change the way in which you serve as a deacon? _____
_____

Do you feel that there is a need for additional ministry in your
ecclesiastical context?

_____ Please explain: _____
Please offer suggestions for improvement and additional information
on reverse.

APPENDIX iiC

Participant Survey for Bishops, Presbyters and Monastics

What jurisdiction are you affiliated? _____

Are you a convert to the Orthodox Church? _____ Previous faith, if so _____

Are you a Bishop or Priest? _____ How long did you serve as a deacon? _____

Have you served in any other Orthodox jurisdictions? _____ Which? _____

Do you serve in a Diocese? _____ Parish? _____ Monastery? _____ Other? _____

When were you tonsured, ordained or consecrated? _____ What is your age? _____

Are you married? _____ Do you have any children? _____ How many? _____

Highest level of education: Grade School _____ College _____ Graduate School _____

Are you a seminary graduate? _____ Seminary_____
Graduation year _____

Did you go through the House of Studies or similar program? _____
Completion date:

Do you consider the diaconate a transitional or permanent
order? _____

Why?_____

Have you allowed a deacon to serve Typika for your
community? _____ Number of Occasions _____ If not, why
not? _____

If so, does he vest? _____ If so, does he cense? _____ If so, does he
preach? _____ If so,

does he compose his own sermons? _____ If so, does he distribute
Holy Communion?

If not, does he lead Vespers w/o a priest or Reader Svs? _____ If so,
with litanies? _____

Has he preached on any other occasions? _____ If so,
when? _____

Does he have occasion to formally teach the faith to others? _____ If
so, on what occasion? _____

Has he ever baptized anyone personally? _____ If so, under what
circumstances?

Has he ever taken the Holy Gifts to hospitals? _____ Shut-ins?
_____ Other? _____

Does he have a Spiritual Father other than his pastor? _____

Does his wife, if married? _____ Does his children, if any? _____

Is he permitted to provide spiritual direction to anyone on a regular basis? _____

Has he ever blessed a religious article or other object? _____ If so, what? _____

Is he an ex-officio member of your parish council as a deacon? _____

Are Subdeacons or Readers eligible to be elected to serve on the parish council? _____

Are their family members eligible to be elected to the parish council? _____

Do your deacons receive any compensation as a clergyman? _____ If so, what? _____

Have deacons in your parish ever attended a National Church Conferences as a delegate?

If so, where they clergy-delegates or a lay-delegates? _____

Have they attended Diocesan Assemblies as a Deacon? _____

Are they considered a clergy delegate at such events? _____

How many services do you expect your deacon to serve on a weekly basis? _____

Are there any aspects of the traditional role of the diaconate that your deacon does that are not mentioned above? If so, please describe: _____

Are there any aspects of the ancient role of the diaconate that you feel are no longer appropriate? If so, which aspects (please state the reason you feel this is so): _____

How will this change the way in which your deacons serve the community? _____
_____

Do you feel that there is a need for additional ministry in your ecclesiastical context?

_____ Please explain: _____
Please offer suggestions for improvement and additional information on reverse.

APPENDIX iii

One-Month Follow-up Survey

Are you a Priest, Deacon, Subdeacon, Reader or
Layman? _____

Jurisdiction_____ State _____
Age _____

No. of families in Parish _____ No. of years as clergyman, if
applicable _____

Cradle or convert _____ Previous Church Affiliation, if
convert _____

1. What part of the conference on *diakonia* (service) stands out in
   your mind the most?
2. Do you think that *diakonia* (active ministry) only applies to
   the priesthood?
3. How concerned should we be about *diakonia*? Is it important
   or are things OK as is?
4. Do you feel that your needs are being served adequately?
5. Do you feel that you are serving the needs of others adequately?
6. What factors did you find contributed most positively to this
   conference?
7. What is your single most valuable insight that you gained from
   the conference?

8. In what ways specifically has the conference changed your ministry or increased your service to Christ in your community?
9. What long-term effect do you think such a conference has for the church – both for the local setting and for the wider church?
10. What personal effect has attending the conference had on you?
11. Was it worth your time, and would you do it again?
12. Do you think the restoration of the ministry of the diaconate would benefit the church or meet the growing needs of the Orthodox in America? If so, why? If not, why not?
13. Do you think that an expanded ministry of the laity and diaconate is faithful to tradition?
14. Do you think that well-trained deacons can serve to strengthen Orthodox unity?
15. Do you think that well-informed laymen and women can serve to bring about Orthodox unity or resolve problems that are common to all Orthodox in America?
16. Did you share information with others after the conference? _____ What?
17. If so, were the conference concepts well received? How so/ Why not?
18. Do you have any comments on the restoration of the ministry of the diaconate?
19. Do you have any comments on the expanded ministerial role of the laity?
20. What do you believe active ministry has to do with your spiritual life?

BiBLiOGRAPhy

Allen, Joseph. "Diaconate" *The Word*. September 1972.

Allen, Joseph J. *The Ministry of the Church: The Image of Pastoral Care.* Crestwood, NY: St. Vladimir's Seminary Press, 1986.

Allen, Joseph J. *Inner Way: Toward a Rebirth of Eastern Christian Spiritual Direction.* Grand Rapids, MI: William B. Eerdmans Publishing Company, 1994.

"Atlanta Resurgens" *The Dawn*, 25, no. 3, (April/May 2002).

Barnett, James Monroe. *The Diaconate: A Full and Equal Order.* Harrisburg, PA: Trinity Press International, 1979.

Church Gazette, 46 (1893) in Nechayev, *Practical Manual for Sacred Ministers.* Moscow, Russia: Sacred Synod of the Russian Orthodox Church, 8th edition, 1903.

Davis, Averky. *Deacon's Manual.* Denver, CO: privately published, 2002.

Dresselhaus, Richard L. *The Deacon and His Ministry.* Springfield, MS: Gospel Publishing House, 1977.

Florovsky, Georges. *The Problem of Diaconate in the Orthodox Church.* http://www.philosophy-religion.org/diaconate/chapter_4.htm, 2006

Hapgood, Isabel Florence, ed. *Service Book of the Holy Orthodox Catholic Church*. Englewood, NJ: Antiochian Christian Orthodox Archdiocese of North America, 1996.

Hussey, J.M. *The Orthodox Church in the Byzantine Empire*. Oxford: Clarendon Press 1986)

Nolan, Richard T. *The Diaconate Now*. Washington D.C: Corpos Books, 1968.

Roshak, Michael Gregory. "The Place of the Diaconate Within The Orthodox Church: M. Div. Thesis, St. Vladimir's Seminary, 1977.

Royster, Dmitri. *Orthodox Christian Teaching*. Syosset, NY: Department of Religious Education, Orthodox Church in America, 1983.

Nicodemus and Agapius of the Holy Mountain, Saints, eds. *The Rudder of the Orthodox Catholic Church*. Chicago, IL: Orthodox Christian Educational Society, 1957

Johannes Quasten. *Patrology: Volumes I – IV*. Utrecht, Holland: Spectrum, 1949: reprint, Allen, TX: Christian Classics, 1957.

Schmemann, Alexander. *Liturgy and Life: Christian Development Through Liturgical Experience*. Syosset, NY: Department of Religious Education, Orthodox Church in America, 1974.

Straub, Gary, and James Trader II. *Your Calling as a Deacon*. St. Louis, MO: Chalice Press, 2005.

Touloumes, Photios. *The Diaconate in the Orthodox Church*. http://hocna.org/orthodox-worship/Diaconate.htm, 2006.

Vlachos, Hierotheos, Metropolitan. *Life After Death*. Levadia, Greece: Birth of the Theotokos Monastery 1995.

Vlachos, Hierotheos, Metropolitan. *Orthodox Psychotherapy: The Science of the Fathers.* Levadia, Greece 1995.

Wallerstedt, Allen, ed. *Orthodox Study Bible.* Nashville, TN: Thomas Nelson Publishers, 1993.

Webb, Henry. *Deacons: Servant Models in the Church.* Nashville, TN: Broadman & Holman Publishers, 2001.

Zizioulas, John D. *Being As Communion.* Crestwood, NY: St. Vladimir's Seminary Press 2002.